Full Circle

Full
Circle

A Play by
Erich Maria Remarque

As adapted by
Peter Stone

Harcourt Brace Jovanovich, Inc., New York

Library of Congress Cataloging in Publication Data
Stone, Peter, 1930–
Full circle.
Adapted from E. M. Remarque's Die letze Station.
I. Remarque, Erich Maria, 1898–1970. Die letze
Station. II. Title.
PS3569.T6416F8   812'.5'4   74–1190
ISBN 0–15–134100–1
ISBN 0–15–634020–8 (pbk.)

A B C D E F G H I J

The Full Circle of
Full Circle

The argument has been put forward that Erich Maria Remarque was the greatest of the German writers whose works were being published between the two World Wars. Kafka was a Czech, Werfel an Austrian; Mann, though German, was primarily a European writer. Remarque wrote about Germany and about war, and for more than thirty years those two subjects were synonymous.

Remarque spent the war years in America, as did so many German writers, and became an American citizen. But his language was German, and after the war he lost no time returning to a country where it was spoken, to Switzerland—because for him it could never again have been Germany.

It was in Switzerland that I first met Erich Remarque, in the spring of 1959. He was living in Ascona, a small village in Ticino, on the shores of the Lago Maggiore. His house was only a few hundred yards from the point where Hemingway had Lieutenant Henry and his Catherine land their small boat after fleeing Italy at the end of *A Farewell to Arms*. It was a magnificent home, filled with the beautiful treasures Erich always wanted around him: paintings by Monet and Van Gogh, Oriental carpets, antique furniture—and his wife, Paulette Goddard.

At the time of our first meeting, five years had passed since Remarque had written his only play, then called *The Last Station*, and seen it successfully produced in Germany. It concerned the lot of three people on the final day of World War II —the widow of a resistance leader, an escaped political prisoner, and a Gestapo officer. I had completed my first adaptation that year, and as it differed considerably from the original, we had many arguments. I was convinced that for an American audience (the winners rather than the losers—a people who had not experienced bombing, shelling, destruction, occupation, starvation, and defeat), the references, identifications, and symbols would have to be either altered, clarified, or reconstructed.

In the end, that first attempt at an American production went by the boards instead of on them. The audience, it was decided, would not be receptive. The war was too recent to be history and too distant to be news.

But now twenty-one years have passed since the creation of *Full Circle*, and its themes—survival, identity, responsibility—are very much in the minds of Americans, who have themselves only recently emerged from a long war and, for the first time in their history, emerged not victorious.

That war has made us question the morality of our own elected government's actions. We learned of atrocities, excesses, intrigues, deceptions; we saw our own soldiers desert and defect; we witnessed an entire people suffering for a cause that *we* held more important than they did. In short, we began to understand, in a frighteningly graphic way, how such a phenomenon as Nazi Germany, and the havoc it had spread, might have been possible.

Survival. Identity. Responsibility. Important subjects for examination following a major conflict—for any nation, for any people, for any person.

Survival. The basic instinct whose priority is so often questioned during times of national struggle. Patriotism, honor, heroism—these are supposed to outrank it. But can the state and its symbols really pre-empt an individual's right to his own life? And is anyone fit to judge who has not undergone the same ordeal?

One's capacity to survive cannot be imagined; it must be

tested. Often it goes hand in hand with one's ability to rationalize. But, then, isn't that the purpose of rationality?
Why shouldn't the POW sign the confession, since everyone will know he didn't mean it?

Identity. As the world becomes more complicated, more mechanized, more automated, the problems of identity become more complex. We have papers, numbers, dossiers. Do these define us? We have clothes, possessions, trappings. Are these our characters? A short man is tall to a midget. A liberal is conservative to a radical. As a character in *Full Circle* says: "What is wet for the cat is dry for the fish."

A Gestapo officer wears the clothes of an escaped concentration camp prisoner—the real prisoner is dressed as a German army officer; the widow of a resistance leader survives on a hero's bonus. When the conflict ends and the slate is wiped clean, will these identities be permanently etched? Do they "take," like a transplanted heart? Or are they "rejected" because of a basic incompatibility with the truth? Or do we have anything whatsoever to do with our own identities? Perhaps they are given to us, formed by the whims and prejudices of others—our friends, our neighbors, our bureaucracy. *Is the draft dodger still a traitor if the cause he fled is discredited?*

Responsibility. Who's to blame—those who made it happen? Or those who let it happen? Or both equally? Those publicly in charge pay a public penalty. But those who silently concurred—or merely went along—what do they owe? And in what strange, private ways will they pay? And from where does forgiveness come?
Does the bombardier's guilt pass up the chain of command until it dissipates or does some portion of it remain forever?

These are vital questions, vital because they arise so often. It is doubtful whether the world has ever really been at peace during the whole of man's recorded history. As one area emerges from the killing and destruction, another submerges; as one people pause to lick their wounds and bury their dead, another launches their attack. Is this, then, the natural activity of man? Do his unique qualities—reason, ambition, fantasy—end irrevocably in conflict?

Does reason imposed on instinct inspire only greed? Does ambition require that climbing up must inevitably accompany a tearing down? Does fantasy conjure anything more than the exercise of power?

These questions cannot be answered now. A postwar atmosphere does not offer sufficient objectivity for optimism. Nor does history offer any evidence that might brighten the outlook. At the moment there can be only a blind faith that any organism as sophisticated as man can eventually control himself.

Certainly he failed miserably in Erich Remarque's time. He has not done much better in ours. But each time man allows a future generation to exist, there must be hope. Without it there seems little point.

—Peter Stone

Full Circle

Cast of Characters
In order of their appearance

ANNA

GRETE

KOERNER

ROHDE

MACK

MAURER

SCHMIDT

KATZ

RUSSIAN SOLDIER

RUSSIAN SERGEANT

RUSSIAN CAPTAIN

Scene One
A third-floor room in Berlin, April 30, 1945

Scene Two
The same, the next morning

The action is continuous, without intermission.

Scene One

A third-floor room in Berlin. There are three doors—one leading to the hall and stairs, another to a closet, the third to the bathroom. There is a bed, a table and chairs, a hot plate, a basin, and a telephone. When the shade is not drawn, the single window looks down on the street in the foreground, and the city in the background; both are in rubble.

TIME

April 30, 1945

AT RISE

The room is dark, the shade drawn. Apparently it is empty. We hear the terrifying sounds of bombing and shelling outside. Now the bombing stops, and the all-clear sirens are heard.

RADIO

Suddenly

This is the Berlin Command Post returning to the air—this is the Berlin Command Post. All clear—repeat—all clear— *Then the phone rings—four times. No one answers it.*

A match strikes and now we can see ANNA's *face—more lifeless than calm; she lies on the bed, wearing a peignoir over a slip. She is twenty-eight and attractive. When the match is blown out we can see only the ember of her cigarette.*

7

Then the door opens and GRETE *enters. Twenty-two, blond, abundantly put together, she has the kind of Wagnerian good looks that border between voluptuousness and fat. She crosses the room to the basin without noticing* ANNA *on the bed. She sets down a kettle and fills it with water. Now she sees the open closet door and crosses to it, leaving the water running. She runs her hands over some dresses, then takes a fur stole off a hanger and drapes it over her shoulders.*

ANNA

Don't you knock any more, Grete?

GRETE

Wheels, terrified

Is—is that you, Frau Walter? I thought you went to the shelter.

ANNA

You'd better turn the water off.

GRETE

Oh—yes—

She crosses to the basin and turns off the water.

Direct hit next door—number seventeen. Now we've got a view to the south—all the way to number eleven.

A pause

I'd like to see the mailman's face tomorrow morning!

ANNA

What do you want, Grete?

GRETE

We haven't any water next door—our pipes burst last night.

ANNA

I thought you might have been cold.

GRETE

Cold? On the last day of April?

Then she notices the fur stole still around her neck.

Oh—

Sheepishly

I saw it in the closet.

ANNA *says nothing.* GRETE *goes to hang it back in the closet.*

I mean—if all it's going to do is hang there it might just as well be back on the mink.

ANNA

A fox fur would look pretty silly on a mink.

RADIO

This is the Berlin Command Post. The enemy raiders have left the capital perimeter and are now heading north, sector Hanover. Repeat—heading north, sector—

ANNA *reaches over and shuts off the radio.*

GRETE

Hey! Why'd you do that? Don't you want to hear the damage reports?

ANNA

No.

A WOMAN'S VOICE

Off

Grete! Grete!

GRETE

Calling off

Just a minute—the water's not boiling yet!

To ANNA

Do you mind if I use the stove? We haven't any electricity either.

She goes to the electric hot plate and snaps it on.

Funny how everything works in here—I mean, if it weren't for the noise you'd hardly know there was a war on.

The phone rings.

You see? Even your telephone!

ANNA *makes no move to answer it.*

Well? Aren't you going to answer it?

ANNA *doesn't move.*

I mean, maybe it's for me. Our phone's out—

She crosses to the phone and lifts the receiver.

ANNA

It's not for you.

Annoyed, she snatches it from GRETE's *hand, looks at it a moment, then lifts it to her ear.*

Yes?— No, he's not here— *He's not here*—he doesn't live here any more— No, there is no other number. He's dead— Two years ago— Who?

A pause as she looks at GRETE

No, I'm not Frau Wilke—

Another pause

—she's dead, too.

She hangs up the phone and lies back on the bed.

GRETE

Who's dead?

ANNA

Nobody.

GRETE

Who's Frau Wilke?

A WOMAN'S VOICE

Off

Grete—Grete—!

GRETE

Goes to door. Calling off

Just a minute, can't you?

Closes door. To ANNA

That pregnant bitch! The way she's got me running day and night—you'd think she's carrying the Führer's child.

ANNA

She's frightened.

GRETE

She's crazy, if you ask me. Didn't you hear her singing that stupid lullaby all during the raid?

ANNA

I don't know—I suppose so.

GRETE

Are you deaf? We could hear it all the way down in the cellar. Who ever heard of singing a lullaby to a baby that's not even born yet?

Staring at ANNA *for a moment*

How come you don't go down to the cellar when the raids start?

Indicating next door with her thumb

ANNA

I'm tired.

GRETE

I'd rather be tired than dead.

ANNA

You're entitled to your opinion.

GRETE

My God! You're not much fun to be with. Maybe if you opened the curtains things wouldn't look so gloomy in here. How come they're closed, anyway? It's broad daylight outside.

She goes to the windows.

ANNA

No, don't!

But GRETE *opens the blinds anyway, flooding the room in light.* GRETE *stares out the window.*

GRETE

My God! Just look at that mess! Still, it's not much worse than yesterday—and the radio said there were only eight thousand casualties yesterday.

ANNA

Go away.

GRETE

What I want to know is what happens now that it's getting warm out? All those dead people buried under all that wreckage—the smell's going to be—

ANNA

Shut up, Grete.

GRETE

Indicating next door again

She says she can hear them at night, scratching, trying to get out. Crazy. It's a miracle that we haven't all gone crazy.

ANNA

Haven't we?

GRETE

Maybe we have and we don't know it. This is the last time I'm ever going to work for anyone who's pregnant. I certainly am glad *I'm* not pregnant.

She thinks a minute, then knocks on wood. She picks up a pair of silk stockings from the back of a chair.

These are real silk, aren't they?

She holds them up.

Real silk! If I had one pair, just one pair, I'd feel like a human being again.

A WOMAN'S VOICE

Off

Grete! What's taking so long?

ANNA

You can have the stockings—just go away.

GRETE

You mean it? I can really have them?

Shots and shouting outside. GRETE *runs to the window.*

Now what's happening?

ANNA

Probably the Russians.

GRETE

She jumps back from the window, startled.

What?

ANNA

Why so surprised? Don't you know they're almost here?

GRETE

She peeks cautiously out the window for a moment, then sighs with relief.

No, it's only the Gestapo, thank God! They seem to be looking for somebody.

She turns and smiles.

Stop trying to scare me—the Russians won't be here today.

ANNA

Tomorrow, then.

GRETE

You sound anxious to see them.

ANNA

I'm anxious for the war to end.

GRETE

Say, you'd better be careful! If old Koerner heard you say that you'd wind up a whole head shorter.

ANNA

Koerner! Why should he care?

GRETE

He's our new block warden.

ANNA

The janitor?

GRETE

Fischer was killed in the raid on Tuesday. So I'd be careful if I were you. You don't want to end up like the Sergeant.

ANNA

What sergeant?

GRETE

Indicating next door

Her husband.

ANNA

I thought he was still at the front.

GRETE

That's what she thinks, too. Promise you won't tell her? The doctor said she shouldn't know—not until after the baby, anyway.

ANNA

What happened?

GRETE

He deserted. He knew about the baby being overdue and tried to get back.

ANNA

Where is he?

GRETE

Downstairs.

ANNA

Why doesn't he come up?

GRETE

Giggling

He can't. He's hanging from the street lamp in front of the house—with a big sign on his chest: "Deserter."

ANNA

Oh, no—

GRETE

Sure. Come look—you can see it from here.

ANNA

Sadly

I can see it just as well from here.

The door opens and KOERNER *enters; he carries a clip board in his hand. Past fifty, his expression is habitually stern, abetted somewhat by the severe way he combs his hair and the sterility of the steel-rimmed glasses he wears.*

KOERNER

Officially

Frau Walter?

ANNA

Doesn't *anybody* knock any more?

KOERNER

I'm the block warden now.

ANNA

I don't care if you're Adolf Hitler now. As long as that door remains standing you'll knock on it.

KOERNER

I have my orders.

He consults his clip board.

Frau Walter—

He checks the list.

—alive.

To GRETE

What are you doing here?

GRETE

I came to get some water.

KOERNER

From now on stay in your own room until the head count has been taken.

GRETE

Saluting

Yes, Herr Field Marshal!

KOERNER

Be careful—you're talking to the representative of the party!

GRETE

Is that what you are? Then maybe you can help capture that escaped madman.

KOERNER

Madman?

GRETE

The one on the radio who keeps saying we're winning the war.

She laughs.

KOERNER

Sharply

Are you criticizing the party?

GRETE

Who, me? That's only a joke I heard in the cellar—

KOERNER

Subversion is punishable by death! We hang traitors every day! Just look out that window if you don't believe me— look at that street lamp down there—

GRETE *tries to silence him.*

GRETE

Shh! Don't forget what the doctor said.

KOERNER

So don't you forget. From now on you will stay in your own room after every raid until *I* take the head count. Is that clear? Heil Hitler!

GRETE

Automatically

Heil Hitler.

KOERNER

Frau Walter, I said Heil Hitler!

ANNA

I heard you.

KOERNER

Why didn't you answer, then?

ANNA

Oh, don't be an idiot.

KOERNER

Apoplectic

What? *What did you say?* You think now that the Russians are close by, you can do any damn thing you please. Well, just wait, all of you! The war's not over yet—the tide will turn, you'll see!

He goes.

GRETE

The silly bastard! Down in the cellar he couldn't keep his horny old hands off my ass, and up here he acts like a member of the High Command.

A pause

The radio says the Russians are all Asiatic subhumans and they'll rape all the women. Do you believe that?

ANNA

Maybe. I don't know.

GRETE

Between the Gestapo hanging everybody and the Russians raping everybody—

ANNA

Why do you suppose they hanged the Sergeant? What difference can a few deserters make now?

GRETE

I don't know—but if all the soldiers just went home, then where would we be?

ANNA

At peace.

GRETE

These are real silk, too, aren't they?

She holds up some underwear.

ANNA

Weary

You can have them, Grete.

GRETE

Really? Oh, you are nice!

A WOMAN'S VOICE

Off

Grete!

GRETE

Calling off

I'm coming!

She picks up the kettle and her new lingerie and starts out.
Now if I get raped at least I'll have some decent-looking underwear.

She giggles and leaves. ANNA *continues to lie on the bed, staring at the ceiling. The telephone rings but she doesn't answer it.*

Then the door opens and ERICH ROHDE *enters. Around thirty, the charm, courage, and attraction of this man have been seriously tampered with; that these qualities are still alive and in evidence speaks well for the degree to which they existed before.* ANNA *hears him but doesn't turn to look.*

ANNA

What do you want now, Grete, more hot water? Why don't you just take the whole stove?

No answer

ROHDE

Coming forward quickly, his hand in his pocket

Don't scream—I have a gun.

ANNA

Calmly

What do you want?

ROHDE

I'm looking for somebody. A man named Wilke—Otto Wilke. He lives here, doesn't he?

ANNA

No.

ROHDE

What do you mean no? He has to live here! They told me number nineteen—third floor—

ROHDE *tries to collect his thoughts while* ANNA *watches him carefully.*

ANNA

I'm sorry. I live here.

ROHDE

But they said *he* lived here.

ANNA

I live here! He used to live here—two years ago.

ROHDE

Two years? They told me only yesterday.

ANNA

News travels slowly these days.

ROHDE

What news?

ANNA

A pause

They took him away.

ROHDE

Who?

ANNA

The Gestapo.

ROHDE

He never came back?

ANNA

Do they ever?

ROHDE

Examining her carefully

Are you related to him?

ANNA

I told you all I know.

ROHDE

Did you know him?

ANNA

You'd better go now.

ROHDE

Sharply

I asked you a question!

ANNA

It's none of your business!

ROHDE

Angrily

You're wrong! It is my business!

A pause

I can make you tell me—

ANNA

With your gun?

ROHDE

Bringing his empty hand out of his pocket

I don't have a gun.

ANNA

I'm sorry, I can't help you. Now get out and leave me alone.

ROHDE *doesn't move and now* ANNA *becomes angry.*

Listen! I don't know who you are and I don't know what you want. All I do know is you can't stay here!

ROHDE

I won't stay long.

ANNA

You won't stay at all.

ROHDE

Haven't you noticed my clothes?

ANNA

Suddenly resigned and weary

When did you escape?

ROHDE

Today—just now. I counted on Otto Wilke's helping me. Someone in prison gave me his name.

ANNA

Too many people knew that name.

ROHDE

But I can't leave the house now—the streets are crawling with Gestapo.

ANNA

What can I do?

ROHDE

Hide me until it gets dark—

ANNA

Did anyone know you were coming here?

ROHDE

Why can't you trust me?

ANNA

You can't trust anybody if you expect to survive.

ROHDE

Sometimes there are more important things than simply surviving.

ANNA

No—surviving is the most important thing there is!

ROHDE

Who told you that?

ANNA

My husband.

ROHDE

Where is your husband?

ANNA

Dead.

ROHDE

I'm sorry.

ANNA

A pause

Were you in a concentration camp?

ROHDE

Yes.

ANNA

Jewish?

ROHDE

No.

ANNA

Politics, then.

ROHDE

Does it matter?

ANNA

No, not to me. How long?

ROHDE

October '38.

ANNA

Seven years. Where?

ROHDE

Buchenwald, mostly. When the Americans got too close they moved us to Oranienburg. Today they brought us here to Berlin.

Looking at her intently

Look, just let me stay here until it gets dark. Then I'll take my chances outside.

A pause

I promise I'll leave when it gets dark—

ANNA

No.

ROHDE

At least I'll have a chance!

ANNA

Not so loud!

ROHDE

A couple of hours—that's not too much to ask!

ANNA

People come in here all the time—without even knocking—

ROHDE

I'll hide in the closet.

ANNA

There's a girl next door who snoops around in there every chance she gets—

ROHDE

Under the bed then—

ANNA

Nobody could get under there—it's too low.

ROHDE

I can do it. Look!

He falls flat and starts to cram himself under the low bed.

ANNA

Pulling him back

Stop it! Get up! How can you make such a fool of yourself? Get up!

Slowly, ROHDE *gets to his feet.*

I want to help you but I can't. I'm afraid! If they find you here they'll hang us both, and I have to stay alive—I have to!

ROHDE

He thinks.

You could say I forced you to hide me.

ANNA

As if she's seen a ghost

What did you say?

ROHDE

You could tell them I forced you.

ANNA

What I tell them is my business, not yours!

ROHDE

I was only trying to protect you—

ANNA

Without warning, she slaps his face.

Who asked you to?

ROHDE *walks away, rubbing his smarting cheek. She looks out the window.*

The street's empty now. You can sneak out.

He starts for the door, then stops and turns.

ROHDE

Don't you at least have something I can wear? One of your husband's suits?

Resigned, she starts rummaging through the dresser. He watches her for a moment, then turns and looks out the window.

ROHDE

Oh, my God.

ANNA

Frightened, she turns.

What is it?

ROHDE

The city—it's nothing but ruins.

ANNA

Have you just now noticed it?

ROHDE

Where do people live?

ANNA

They don't.

She has come up with a uniform—trousers, shirt, and boots.

Here. Put these on.

He looks but does not take them.

ROHDE

Whose are they?

ANNA

Does it matter?

ROHDE

Your husband's?

ANNA

Take them or don't take them. But don't cross-examine me!

ROHDE

Taking the clothes

I didn't mean to. I'm sorry.

ANNA

And don't apologize, either.

She goes to the bed and lies down. ROHDE *begins changing his clothes.*

ROHDE

After an air raid, everything's so quiet. That was the worst part about prison—the awful silence. The raids were the only thing that kept us from going mad. When the bombing started they let us out into the corridor. We could talk because the guards couldn't hear us—we learned to do it without moving our lips. That's where I first heard about Otto Wilke—two days ago. Somebody kept repeating his name and address over and over again, close to my ear. I don't know who it was. He was standing right behind me but I couldn't see him—we weren't allowed to move. We couldn't even move our heads—

ANNA

I don't want to hear about it.

ROHDE

Early this morning they came to get us. They put us in trucks and brought us to Berlin, to the zoo. No irony intended—it was just convenient. They said they were going to let us go, and everybody believed it. We knew it wasn't true, but we believed it anyway. Then they started to shoot—one group at a time.

ANNA *turns away in disgust.*

It was the air raid that saved us. When the bombing started we ran. We scattered in all directions, like chickens on a highway. Some went behind the reptile house, some into the camel enclosure—I saw one man die in the seal tank, can you imagine? When we got to the city streets we kept running until we got lost among all the other people who were running, too. Everybody was running but you could tell the escaped prisoners—they weren't looking up at the planes like the others. They were looking back over their shoulders—and running just a little faster. The whole time I kept repeating the instructions that disembodied voice whispered in my ear: "Wilke, Otto Wilke. He'll help you. Go to the Kurfürstendamm, then the second street after the

Brandenburgerstrasse—twice to the right, number nineteen, third floor. Wilke, Otto Wilke. He'll help you—"

ANNA

Forget about Wilke! He can't help you now—he couldn't even help himself! We've all got to forget about Wilke!

ROHDE

Why?

ANNA

Because he lived here and they caught him—because he's dead and buried and useless!

ROHDE

He is dressed now.

It fits pretty well. But the boots are too tight.

ANNA

Forgive me.

ROHDE

Where's the tunic?

ANNA

I don't know. I don't have it.

ROHDE

I can't go outside half dressed!

ANNA

What do you suggest?

ROHDE

A pause

At least let me stay until it's dark.

ANNA

All right—but that's all.

ROHDE

Handing her his old clothes

You'd better hide these somewhere—I'll be needing them again.

ANNA

Why?

ROHDE

I don't want to be wearing this uniform when the Russians get here.

ANNA

So that's what it all comes down to—the right suit of clothes.

She goes to the dresser and gets a pistol.

Here—you'll probably need this, too.

ROHDE

Examining it

It's not loaded. Do you have any ammunition?

ANNA

No.

ROHDE

Then what good is it?

ANNA

Shrugging

It looks loaded, doesn't it? All guns look loaded. I don't suppose you have any false papers?

ROHDE

No.

ANNA

Then you'll have to say you lost them.

ROHDE

Unless they search me, of course.

ANNA

Why? What will they find?

ROHDE

Unbuttoning his left sleeve and showing a tattooed number

My real papers.

ANNA

Staring at it; finally

You're finished if anyone sees that.

ROHDE

What do you suggest?

ANNA

Please go now—

ROHDE

You said I could stay until dark.

ANNA

Not with that—

ROHDE

Looking at it, too

It won't wash off, I'm afraid.

A pause; his tone changes.

Actually, the time may come when these things could be pretty valuable. After all, how many will there be left? And the work is first rate—they say the tattoo artists were recruited from the docks of Hamburg and Bremerhaven. Mine must've been a little drunk, though. Look at this seven. It looks more like a nine—

ANNA

Distraught

Please—just go—

ROHDE

Is that coffee on the stove? I wouldn't mind a cup of something warm.

ANNA

No, it's just water. If I fix you some tea, will you leave afterward?

ROHDE

Oh, please, let me do it! I haven't done it in so long. I used to make the best cup of tea in town—even my English friends used to say so.

He goes to the stove and begins puttering with a teapot, a tin of leaf tea, cups, spoons, and saucers, his back to the audience all the time. These activities are accompanied by a steady stream of small talk as he carries on both ends of a conversation, supplying her words as well as his own.

(*She:*) Oh, did you have some English friends? How interesting! How did you happen to meet them?

(*He:*) Well, it's nice of you to ask. I went to school for a year in England.

(*She:*) You don't say! You are a fascinating fellow, aren't you? May I ask what you studied?

(*He:*) You certainly may—the metaphysical poets of the seventeenth century. George Herbert, Thomas Traherne, John Donne—"Stay, O sweet, and do not rise! / The light that shines comes from thine eyes; / The day breaks not, it is my heart, / Because that you and I must part—"

He stops.

ANNA

She has been listening.

Go on, finish it.

When he doesn't, she turns and sees that he is standing, his shoulders hunched, his body tense, his head bowed, straining and trembling.

What's wrong—are you ill?

No answer

What is it?

She rushes to him and sees whatever it is he's been doing.

Oh, my God! Stop it—*stop it!*

She grabs at his arm and pulls it away.

Your arm—you've burned off the skin!

ROHDE

Panting from the ordeal

I told you it wouldn't wash off—

ANNA

Why did you do it?

Quietly; her attitude toward him has changed.

You fool—you damn fool. Come here. Sit down so I can

bandage it. There isn't any butter—I'll have to use cold cream.

ROHDE

A funny world—no food but plenty of cosmetics—

She has gone to a dressing table to get bandages and a jar of cream, and now returns to him and starts applying these to his arm.

ANNA

What a mess—

ROHDE

Wouldn't it be funny if my skin grew back with the number still on it—as if it had become part of my genetic structure.

ANNA

Why did you do it?

ROHDE

I had no choice. You were right—it *was* too dangerous. And I have to be sure—

ANNA

Sure of what?

ROHDE

That someone gets away—even if there's only one—to be a witness for all the others who didn't make it, so that everyone knows what happened there and who's to blame.

ANNA

Vengeance.

ROHDE

Yes! Why not?

ANNA

But then you'll be as guilty as they are.

ROHDE

I am guilty.

ANNA

Are you?

ROHDE

Yes, I saw it coming, I smelled the smoke—why didn't I shout "Fire"?

ANNA

She has finished the bandaging.

But they put you in prison—you must've done something.

ROHDE

Yes—in 1938! But why did I wait so long? For six years I just watched it happen and did nothing, like everybody else. I was too busy, you see, working as a ghost writer for celebrities who weren't up to writing their own stories—film stars, football players, condemned murderers. I ground out my four thousand irrelevant words a day and nursed my investments. Then I heard about the camps. I didn't believe it at first—I *couldn't.* Then a friend told me about the ovens, about the children being put in like loaves of bread. That's the way he put it—like loaves of bread. I couldn't erase that picture from my mind. I couldn't look at a loaf of bread without feeling sick. I couldn't sleep at night. Finally I wrote a letter asking if it were true. That's all—a letter! To the editor of the *Berliner Tageblatt.* But it was never printed. Two days later I was arrested by the Gestapo. They asked me why I'd written the letter, why I was asking questions, why I was interfering in things that were none of my business. I told them it was my business, that I was a German and if Germany were doing such things that it was very much my business.

A pause

Do you know what they did then? They made me *eat* my letter—that's right, they tore it up and forced me to swallow every shred of it! All of my indignation and eloquence —it tasted so dry and stale. And when I threw it up they made me swallow it again. I was meant to *digest* it, you see, and eliminate it—that was the whole point!

Another pause

Yes, I am guilty—for waiting until it was too late, for allowing them to accumulate their power. They'll tell you it grew from their strength, but it's a lie. It came from our neglect.

ANNA

How do you feel?

ROHDE

Rotten.

ANNA

I have some brandy.

ROHDE

No, it would only make me sick. I'm not used to alcohol.

ANNA

Then come lie down.

ROHDE

Just until it gets dark.

ANNA

A pause

Until it's safe for you to leave.

She helps him lie down.

ROHDE

Thank you—

He closes his eyes.

—it's been a long time since I said that—

A knock at the door. He tries to sit up.

What's that?

ANNA

I don't know. Lie back—I'll take care of it.

She opens the door. GRETE *enters, then stops short when she sees* ROHDE.

GRETE

Oh! Excuse me. I didn't know anyone—

ANNA

Indifferently

My cousin.

GRETE

Your cousin! Really?

Smiling, she stares at ROHDE *for a moment.*

Well, I don't want to intrude on a family reunion.

ANNA

You're not intruding, Grete. Hans got here last night.

GRETE

Smelling gossip

Last night?

ANNA

Yes. Didn't you hear him come up the stairs?

GRETE

No. And why didn't I see him when I was in here before?

ANNA

Is there any particular reason why he should report his movements to you?

GRETE

Flustered

No, I—

ANNA

You must stop asking so many questions.

GRETE

I'm sorry—I won't do it any more. Is he on leave, or a deserter?

ANNA

Really, you're impossible! He's not a deserter, if you must know, he's just passing through on his way from the west front to the east.

GRETE

Giggling

They say you can do that on the subway these days.

ANNA

Was there something you wanted, Grete?

GRETE

A few towels, that's all—just some towels.

ANNA *goes to the cabinet and returns with the towels. She hands them to* GRETE.

Well, I guess I'll be going now—

At a loss

Uh, will he be staying long?

ANNA

Next you'll be asking to see his travel orders.

GRETE

Routed

No—no, I won't— I'm sorry I— Thanks for the towels.

She beats a hasty retreat, closing the door after her.

ROHDE

That wasn't very smart, telling her I spent the night.

ANNA

I didn't want her to think you just arrived, in case she hears about the escaped prisoners.

ROHDE

It was smart.

GRETE *enters again, without knocking.*

GRETE

There's a Gestapo patrol searching the house—looking for some escaped prisoners, I think.

ROHDE

Did you call them?

GRETE

Me? Are you crazy? Who wants the Gestapo poking around?

She thinks about his question.

Why? Are you hiding something?

ANNA

Curtly

Of course not. Is there anything else, Grete?

GRETE

Isn't that enough?

She smiles and moves to the door.

Well—good luck, *cousin.*

She leaves.

ANNA

That wasn't very smart, asking if she called them.

She crosses to him and removes his boots, then hands him the gun.

Put this under the pillow. Now listen. You were here last night—with me—understand? Your name's Vollmer. Hans Vollmer. You were born in Breslau. You're a lieutenant in the Artillery.

ROHDE

Who's Vollmer?

ANNA

He was killed in North Africa three years ago.

ROHDE

Was this his uniform?

ANNA

Will you stop wasting time?

ROHDE

They'll check—

ANNA

They can't. Breslau's in Russian hands.

She hurriedly puts lipstick on, then grabs his face between her hands and kisses him, smearing some of her lipstick on him. She goes right on talking, rapidly and frantically.

ROHDE

Where have I been stationed?

ANNA

Rostock.

ROHDE

Formation?

ANNA

JR 27.

She grabs a brandy bottle.

You were in the hospital—

ROHDE

JR 27—

ANNA

You lost your papers—you were drunk—you're still
drunk—

She hands him the bottle.

I can hear them on the stairs!

He drinks and chokes. He has a coughing fit.

ROHDE

We can't fool them—nobody can—

ANNA

Forcefully

We will! We'll lie—we'll lie about everything—we'll lie
our heads off— Lie down.

She lies down next to him. There's a moment's silence.

ROHDE

Suddenly

My God! Your name! I don't know your name!

ANNA

Whispering loudly

Anna Walter.

The door bursts open. MACK *and* MAURER, *two uniformed
Gestapo men, enter with drawn guns. In his middle
twenties,* MACK *has allowed his constant disapproval of most
things to distort his face into a perpetual sneer.*

Older, thirtyish, MAURER *is large and stupid. He rarely, if
ever, speaks, but the acts of inhuman brutality that consti-
tute his duty and his pleasure form the great equalizer.*

The two soldiers are followed by CAPTAIN SCHMIDT. *In his
early thirties, he is a man of intelligence, wit, and some at-
tractiveness. He is educated and articulate, but he is neither
an intellectual nor a fanatic—merely an opportunist.*

MACK

Speaking as he enters

Nobody move!

ROHDE *pretends to sleep.*

ANNA

Sitting up

That's right, don't knock—just walk in! Everybody does!

SCHMIDT

Quiet please. Heil Hitler!

Saluting

ANNA

Heil Hitler.

SCHMIDT

Group Leader Captain Schmidt. Your name?

ANNA

Smiling

Anna Walter.

SCHMIDT

Indicating that MACK *should write it down*

Walter—Anna. Married?

ANNA

My husband's dead.

SCHMIDT

My condolences.

ANNA

You're a little late—he's been dead two years.

SCHMIDT

Who's he?

ANNA

You'd better ask him.

SCHMIDT

I'm asking you.

MACK

He's drunk, Captain—the whore, too. I can smell it from here.

ANNA

Do I have to stand for that?

SCHMIDT

I suppose so.

ROHDE

He stirs.

Please, I'm trying to sleep.

SCHMIDT

Maurer—

MAURER *goes to* ROHDE *quickly; he roughly pulls him to a sitting position.*

ROHDE

Dazed

What's going on here?

ANNA

Bravo! One insults defenseless women and the other attacks wounded soldiers! Why aren't they out fighting Russians?

MACK

Shut your mouth!

ROHDE

Oh, Christ—my head! Do you have to shout?

MACK

Let Maurer teach this drunk some manners, Captain.

ROHDE

Be careful who you call a drunk, soldier. There may not be much of an army left, but an officer still outranks a—

He squints at MACK's *sleeve.*

—a sergeant.

SCHMIDT

You're an officer?

ROHDE

First lieutenant! Can't you see?

ANNA

Laughing

How do you expect him to see your rank if you're not wearing your tunic?

ROHDE

What?

Laughing

Please forgive me, Captain. Have a cognac?

No reaction from SCHMIDT

No? Well, I could use one. Anna, get me a cognac—my mouth feels like a gravel pit.

He looks around the room unsteadily.

Where the hell's my tunic?

ANNA

Don't you remember?

ROHDE

I wouldn't be asking if I remembered, would I?

SCHMIDT

I hope one of you remembers.

ANNA

He threw it out the window!

ROHDE

I didn't!

He stops, looks at ANNA.

I did? I must have really been pissed!

ANNA

Watch your language!

SCHMIDT

Yes—we mustn't offend the lady.

To ANNA

You say he threw his tunic out the window? Why?

ANNA

He wanted to cover the head of that deserter hanging on the lamppost down there.

ROHDE

Deserter—? Yes, I grew sick of looking at him.

ANNA

I went down to get it after the raid but it was gone!

SCHMIDT

I'm sure it was.

ANNA

Excuse me, but are we being accused of something?

SCHMIDT

Have I said so?

ANNA

You're treating us like common criminals.

ROHDE

Anna, please. I'm sure the Group Leader didn't come here
to arrest us for having a few drinks—

SCHMIDT

We're looking for escaped prisoners.

ANNA

You expect to find them here?

SCHMIDT

I expect to find them anywhere.

ANNA

Then look around, Group Leader—you can see for yourself
there are no escaped prisoners here. You can go now.

SCHMIDT

Smiling

I'm perfectly willing to take orders from a lady—but only
off duty.

To ROHDE

May I see your papers, please, Lieutenant?

ANNA

Quickly

Tell me, Group Leader—what do these prisoners of yours
look like?

SCHMIDT

They're not mine yet, Frau Walter. Why do you ask—have
you seen them?

ANNA

Smiling

I won't know that until you tell me what they look like. Are
they wearing prison clothes?

SCHMIDT

Yes, of course—at least, they were.

ANNA

Were? What are they wearing now?

SCHMIDT

Who knows? It might be almost anything. A business suit—
an army uniform—

ANNA

Or a Gestapo uniform—

SCHMIDT

One of them's quite dangerous—he killed a man.

ANNA

Surprised

Killed?

SCHMIDT

Yes. Grabbed him by the throat and broke his neck.

ANNA

That's quite a stunt. He must have been pretty large—like
your helper there.

Indicating MAURER

Can't he talk?

SCHMIDT

Maurer? He has other talents.

MAURER *grins broadly.*

But I hope you'll never find out what they are—you're much
too attractive.

ANNA

No, no—not at the moment, I'm not. I must look awful.

She checks herself in a compact and winces.

Holy Christ! At least let me fix my face!

She begins applying lipstick.

MACK

Lipstick is un-German!

41

ANNA

Then don't use it.

She crosses to the closet, where she will change into a dress.

SCHMIDT

Turning to ROHDE

All right, Lieutenant, for the record—name?

ROHDE

With military precision

Vollmer, Hans, First Lieutenant, JR 27, Rostock. Discharged yesterday from the hospital. Ambulant. Orders to report back tonight at nineteen-hundred hours.

SCHMIDT

Thank you. Papers?

ROHDE

Certainly. Papers—papers—papers—

He begins groping through his trouser pockets.

Anna, where's my wallet?

ANNA

How's that?

ROHDE

My wallet—where is it?

ANNA

Meaning what?

ROHDE

Getting angry

Meaning I can't find it!

ANNA

Meaning *I* took it?

ROHDE

I didn't say that! But I had it when I came up here—

ANNA

Isn't that wonderful! First he swills all my liquor and now he calls me a pickpocket! Get out of here!

ROHDE

Anna, please. All of my papers—all my identification—

SCHMIDT

Wearily

I don't suppose they could have been in your tunic—

ROHDE *puts his hand to his head.*

ANNA

Oh, really? You mean I didn't steal them after all? Thank you very much! I'm sick of looking at you—get out!

SCHMIDT

Please, Frau Walter. I'll decide who leaves and when.

ROHDE

Forgive me, Anna.

SCHMIDT

Perhaps there are other ways of verifying your identity, Lieutenant— What's wrong with your arm?

ROHDE

You can see for yourself—I was wounded.

SCHMIDT

I'm afraid I cannot see for myself unless you remove the dressing.

ANNA

Oh, please, not in here, if you don't mind!

ROHDE

Don't worry. I have no intention of publicly displaying my wounds. I was burned by a shell casing, Captain. I insist that you take my word for it.

ANNA

Now I've heard everything! A lieutenant insisting to a captain?

ROHDE

Yes—an army lieutenant to a police captain.

ANNA

To SCHMIDT

Will you stand for that, Captain? Maybe he can push me around, but you—

SCHMIDT

Please, be quiet! Which hospital, Lieutenant—the name.

ROHDE

A pause

I don't understand the reason for all these questions!

SCHMIDT

The name of the hospital, Lieutenant—

ANNA

As ROHDE *again hesitates*

I don't mind telling you, Group Leader. It was Hedwig Military. He told me so.

To ROHDE

That will teach you to accuse me of things.

SCHMIDT

He looks from one to the other, not sure what's going on.

Mack—

MACK

Snapping to attention

Captain!

SCHMIDT

Call Hedwig Hospital.

To ANNA

Is your phone working?

ANNA

I doubt it.

MACK

He picks up the receiver, listens, then grins.

It works, Captain.

He dials the operator.

Hedwig Hospital, Fräulein— What?— I don't know the number— I don't *have* a telephone book! Fräulein—
Fräulein, listen— *Fräulein!* This is official business—
Gestapo business— Thank you, Fräulein.

Covering the mouthpiece

She's getting it, Captain.

SCHMIDT

To ROHDE

What was the name of your doctor?

ROHDE

Sorry, he didn't introduce himself.

MACK

Into the phone

Hello? Hedwig Hospital?— What? I don't—I can't understand— Who's this?

SCHMIDT

Impatiently

Give it to me, you idiot! Can't you make a simple phone
call?

Takes the phone

Group Leader Captain Schmidt speaking. Give me Admis-
sions, please— What? What are you saying?— I don't understand you—

Slowly he lowers the receiver.

ANNA

What did they say?

SCHMIDT

I don't know. I don't speak Russian.

ANNA

Only two miles away—not very far, is it, Group Leader?
An hour perhaps?

SCHMIDT

Or a week.

ANNA

Well, whichever it is, I feel much safer with the Gestapo
here. You will defend us against those Asiatic subhumans,
won't you, Group Leader?

Suddenly, MAURER *moves noiselessly to the door and yanks it open.* GRETE *almost stumbles into the room.*

GRETE

Lamely

May I have a few more towels, Frau Walter?

SCHMIDT

Who's this?

ANNA

She works next door—for Frau Zandler.

SCHMIDT

Who's Frau Zandler?

GRETE

She's expecting a baby. Two weeks overdue—

SCHMIDT

Why were you listening at the door?

GRETE

I wasn't listening. I was about to knock—

SCHMIDT

With your ear?

GRETE

Anxious to shift attention from herself, she turns to ANNA.

What's wrong, Frau Walter? Is your *cousin* in trouble?

SCHMIDT

Turning to ROHDE

Cousin?

ANNA

You know how it is during wartime, Group Leader—no acquaintances but many friends, no family but many cousins.

GRETE

With satisfaction

That's what I thought. Why else would he spend the night?

SCHMIDT

He spent the night here last night?

GRETE

And that's not all. They didn't go down to the cellar during the raid and it doesn't take a genius to figure out why.

ANNA

Quietly

That's enough, Grete.

SCHMIDT

He thinks for a moment, staring at ROHDE *all the time.*

Maurer—

MAURER *jumps to attention.*

Go downstairs and bring up the prisoner.

MAURER *salutes smartly, does an about-face, and leaves the room.*

We caught one of them alive.

ANNA

Is there any particular reason for this?

SCHMIDT

Probably not.

A silence

ROHDE

Tell me, Captain—have you actually seen the prisoners yourself?

SCHMIDT

Why do you ask?

ROHDE

I thought perhaps you could describe them to us—so we could watch out for them.

GRETE

Yes—what do they look like?

SCHMIDT

After a few years in the camp, they don't look like anything.

A silence

GRETE

Chattering nervously

Well, I just think it's wonderful the way you people go

about your business—I mean, with the Russians so close, and all. I mean, you Gestapo people are in such terrible danger—

SCHMIDT

Oh? Why's that?

GRETE

Everybody hates the Gestapo.

SCHMIDT

Smiling faintly

Really?

GRETE

Realizing what she's said

Our enemies, I mean. Naturally *we* don't—

She sees the expression on SCHMIDT's *face and looks around for a way out.*

Let's see if there's any news.

She turns on the radio.

RADIO

—resisting fiercely. The Russians have broken through to the inner city according to one report. Zeitz' Department Store has been abandoned, as well as the Friedrichstadt subway station. In the Wilmersdorf sector Russian tanks have been steadily advancing and are at this moment shelling the—

SCHMIDT

That's enough of that.

GRETE

Turning off the radio

Yes—the news on that station is always bad.

ANNA

Keep on trying. Maybe you'll find a station where we're winning.

MACK

That's subversive! Don't you know we shoot people who make subversive statements?

ANNA

Winning the war subversive?

MACK

But we're *not* winning!

ANNA

That's subversive! Shoot yourself!

MACK

Confused

What?

SCHMIDT

I'm afraid you're no match for her, Mack.

The door opens and MAURER *returns pushing the prisoner,* KATZ, *before him. In his middle fifties,* KATZ *is dressed in prison clothes; he is bleeding and seems weak and exhausted.*

MACK

To KATZ

Attention!

No reaction from KATZ; MAURER *kicks him and he straightens up a little.*

SCHMIDT

Tell us your name.

KATZ

Reciting

Prisoner in protective custody, number 87112.

MAURER *kicks him again.*

Prisoner in protective custody, number 87112, *sir.*

SCHMIDT

I asked for your name.

KATZ

Prisoner in protective custody—

MACK

Screaming

Your *name!*

49

KATZ

Automatically

I'm a dirty Jewish swine.

SCHMIDT

Patiently, almost bored

Your name—your real name.

KATZ

Hesitating

I am Izzy—a dirty Jewish swine.

GRETE

Why won't he tell his name?

SCHMIDT

Nobody's going to hurt you—you're not in prison now. Tell us your real name.

KATZ

Apprehensive

Katz—

SCHMIDT

Very good. And your Christian name?

KATZ

Christian name? Joseph—

SCHMIDT

Joseph Katz. All right. Profession?

KATZ

Pausing to think

I'm a dirty Jewish—

SCHMIDT

Besides that, you idiot! What did you do before?

MACK

Circumciser in the synagogue.

GRETE *snickers.*

KATZ

I was Doctor Joseph Katz, professor of chemistry, lieutenant in the reserve, holder of the Iron Cross, first and second class—

He stops.

SCHMIDT

Go on—

KATZ

—and a dirty Jewish swine.

SCHMIDT

He stares at KATZ *for a moment.*

Very well. Now, I want the answers to a few simple questions. Do you understand?

KATZ

Yes.

SCHMIDT

I want to know where you were going when you were captured, whom you were going to see, and the whereabouts of the man who escaped with you, Erich Rohde. Nothing else. Is that clear?

KATZ

Yes.

SCHMIDT

Softly

Katz, where were you going?

KATZ

Nowhere.

SCHMIDT

Whom were you looking for?

KATZ

No one.

SCHMIDT

Where is Erich Rohde?

KATZ

I don't know Erich Rohde.

SCHMIDT

Do you know anyone in this room?

KATZ

He looks from face to face, slowly, coming finally to ROHDE.

No one.

GRETE

My! That was exciting, wasn't it?

SCHMIDT

Do you know that one of you strangled a guard, Katz? Was it you?

KATZ

No.

SCHMIDT

Then it was Rohde.

KATZ

I don't know any Rohde, Group Leader.

SCHMIDT

I can promise you will by tomorrow, Katz. It would be much easier to tell me now.

No answer

It seems that you're an intelligent man, Katz—as far as that's possible for one of your race—so I presume you know what's going to happen to you?

KATZ

Yes, Group Leader. I will be questioned further and then liquidated.

SCHMIDT

That's correct. So we'll strike a bargain, eh, Katz? Tell me where I can find Erich Rohde and there'll be no more questioning.

KATZ

No more questioning?

SCHMIDT

I promise you'll be shot immediately.

ANNA

What sort of a bargain is that?

MACK

Quiet!

SCHMIDT

To ANNA

You think it's unfair? Katz, would you rather be questioned or shot?

KATZ

Shot, Group Leader.

SCHMIDT

Of course. All right, where is Erich Rohde?

KATZ

I don't know Erich Rohde, Group Leader.

SCHMIDT

A pause; he thinks.

Katz, how would you like to go free?

KATZ

Free?

SCHMIDT

Speaking quietly

Yes, Katz, free! That sounds quite different, doesn't it?

KATZ *says nothing.*

Don't be a fool, Katz. The war may be over soon—why throw your life away now when you've come so close?

KATZ *says nothing.*

Well? What do you say?

KATZ

They promised to set us free this morning, too—

SCHMIDT

But this is different! I want the man who murdered the guard. I'm willing to pay for it. The moment we have him we'll set you free, Katz. I give you my word.

GRETE

To KATZ

Why don't you tell him? No one will ever know—

SCHMIDT

That's right, Katz. Besides, he'll probably be caught anyway. Why should you suffer for him? An Aryan—a *goy*. Now, which will it be, Katz? Do I set you free, or do I turn you over to Maurer there?

KATZ

When—when the air raid began we all started running—in the direction of the Kurfürstendamm—

SCHMIDT

That's it—go on—

KATZ

—in the direction of the Kurfürstendamm. I looked back a few times—one or two were behind me. When I got to the Weidendamm Bridge the bombs started dropping all around me—I fell down—I stayed down until the bombing stopped. When I got up I didn't see anybody— The others must have been killed—must have been killed—

He trails off.

SCHMIDT

Go on, Katz.

KATZ

That's all, Group Leader.

A silence

GRETE

It sounds believable to me—

MACK

Shut up!

SCHMIDT

Turns to GRETE

There's a pregnant woman next door. The Jew's screaming might upset her. Turn the radio up, please.

GRETE *hesitates, then turns up the radio.*

RADIO

—advancing along a wide front in the northern sector. Meanwhile, to the south, the American armies are encountering—

SCHMIDT

Maurer, break his fingers.

MAURER *advances menacingly.*

RADIO

The voice breaks off; a new one continues.

Attention! Attention! This is the Berlin Command Post. The enemy has advanced within three hundred meters of the Führer's bunker. Repeat—three hundred meters from the Führer's bunker—

Taking advantage of the shift of attention, KATZ *breaks for the open window and has jumped up onto the sill before anyone can stop him.* MACK *and* MAURER *draw their guns.*

MACK

The Jew's escaping!

SCHMIDT

Don't shoot! I want him alive!

MACK

He can't get away! It's three floors straight down!

SCHMIDT

Leave him alone!

MACK

But he's bluffing, Captain!

SCHMIDT

Quiet!

KATZ

You be quiet.

The unexpected force of his voice silences everyone.

You're finished—all of you—caught in a trap like your Führer—all the murderers, the cowards, the thieves, the criminals, the liars—the ones who break bones and open veins and abuse children—you're finished, all of you—

SCHMIDT

Screaming

Katz! Come down from there! That's an order!

KATZ

You're through giving orders to me! Don't you think I knew all those promises of yours were lies?

SCHMIDT

They weren't, Katz—I give you my word.

KATZ

Beg me, Group Leader—*plead* with me—

MACK

Let me finish him, Captain—

SCHMIDT

No! You can't escape, Katz. We can wait.

KATZ

Good. So can I. We'll wait for the report.

SCHMIDT

What report?

KATZ

The news that he's dead—that the pig is dead. Didn't you hear? Only three hundred meters—

MACK

Let me shoot him now, Group Leader!

SCHMIDT

No! I want him alive. All right, Maurer, get him.

MAURER *advances slowly toward the window.*

KATZ

No, wait—a moment longer—can't you wait a moment longer? He's not dead yet—

MAURER *moves closer.*

—the pig's not dead yet! Now I'll never know—

This last quietly and sadly as he lets himself fall backward, down, out of sight. MAURER *makes a desperate lunge but he is too late.*

GRETE *screams. Then silence*

SCHMIDT

Suddenly barking orders to MACK *and* MAURER

Quick—downstairs! Maybe he's still alive!

MACK *and* MAURER *hurry out.* GRETE *has moved to the window and is looking down at the street.* SCHMIDT *joins her.* ANNA *and* ROHDE *stay where they are, staring at each other.*

What could I do? The idiot was determined to jump—I couldn't stop him.

GRETE

What are you going to do now?

SCHMIDT

Blowing up

How the hell does that concern you?

GRETE

I was only—

SCHMIDT

He shouts down to MACK *and* MAURER.

Is he dead?— Are you sure?— Well, make sure, God damn it!

Mocking, to the others

They *think* so! What makes them think they can think?

He takes out his handkerchief and dries his face and neck.

Oh, what's the difference! What's another Shylock more or less in this world?

ANNA

He was a professor of chemistry.

SCHMIDT

Or a professor, for that matter. Still, it would have been better to have kept him alive. Now they'll blame *me* for it—

To ROHDE

Won't they, Lieutenant?

No answer

I said, *Won't they, Lieutenant?*

ROHDE

Won't they what?

SCHMIDT

Blame me!

57

ROHDE

I don't know—how the hell should I know?

GRETE

Now, if you'd've tied up his hands and feet he couldn't have jumped—

SCHMIDT

Will you shut up!

The radio, which has been left on, suddenly blares.

RADIO

The voice is solemn.

This is Radio Berlin returning to the air. Here in the head-quarters of the High Command we have just learned of the tragic death of our beloved Führer. He died heroically in the fulfillment of his duty. We repeat—our glorious leader, Adolf Hitler, is dead. Grand Admiral Doenitz has assumed command and will continue the valiant defense of our Fatherland. We will now play the Funeral March from Wagner's *Götterdämmerung*.

The music begins.

ANNA

After a moment

He's—dead?

SCHMIDT

They must have murdered him.

GRETE

Who?

SCHMIDT

The generals, of course—didn't they try before?

GRETE

It looks like the end now—without the Führer—

SCHMIDT

Doenitz—a navy man—why not Himmler? Why did they pass up Himmler?

ROHDE

Maybe he's dead, too.

SCHMIDT

Maybe—yes, that's probably it. Well—

He walks to the window and looks down at the street below.

—no one's likely to ask many questions about the Jew, not with the Führer dead.

GRETE

That's one consolation. Well, I'd better get back to Frau Zandler before she starts hollering.

She goes to the door.

SCHMIDT

Absent-mindedly

Yes—I'll go with you—got to finish searching the building.

GRETE

Nobody's hidden in *our* room.

SCHMIDT

No, I suppose not. Himmler couldn't be dead—the radio would have mentioned it. Then why Doenitz?

Turning to ANNA *and* ROHDE

You two think you got away with something, but you didn't. I don't know what your game is, but there's something fishy about it.

To ROHDE

When are you going back?

ROHDE

Tonight.

SCHMIDT

See that you do—or they'll string you up on the lamppost like that sergeant down there.

To ANNA

Did they say how the Führer died?

ANNA

Heroically—in the fulfillment of his duty.

SCHMIDT

Yes, yes, but *how?*

ANNA

They didn't say.

SCHMIDT

They did say Doenitz, didn't they?

ANNA

Yes.

SCHMIDT

I wonder what it means. He's not even a party member—

To ANNA

You're a smart girl.

He looks at ROHDE *briefly, then smiles at* ANNA.

Who knows? We might even meet again someday.

To GRETE, *his manner suddenly changing*

Come on.

SCHMIDT *and* GRETE *exit.* ROHDE *and* ANNA *are left alone. Dusk is approaching. The Funeral March plays on.*

ANNA

She goes to the door and listens.

It's all right—he's next door—talking to Frau Zandler.

She turns back to ROHDE *and studies him for a moment.*

Your name is Erich Rohde.

ROHDE

Yes.

ANNA

The Jew knew you, didn't he?

ROHDE

Yes.

ANNA

And he didn't betray you—

ROHDE

No.

ANNA

Why?

ROHDE

Would it have saved him?

ANNA

It might have. You never know.

ROHDE

No.

ANNA

Louder

You never know, I tell you! That music—as if we were dead, too!

She turns off the radio.

You killed the guard?

ROHDE

Yes.

ANNA

They taught you pretty well.

ROHDE

It doesn't need teaching. It's the simplest thing in the world.

Shaking his head

Not killing, that's what takes character.

SCHMIDT

Off

Your husband was a traitor, a deserter!

A WOMAN'S VOICE is heard, off, wailing pitifully.

ROHDE

The bastard! The filthy bastard!

ANNA

Shh! We mustn't betray ourselves now.

They are close and looking into one another's eyes. It is dark except for the red glow of a burning building outside.
GRETE enters.

GRETE

He's gone.

ANNA

Did he find anything?

GRETE

Of course not. He's crazy, you know. I think the Führer's death was too much for him. I warned him not to tell Frau Zandler about her husband, but he told her deliberately. It was terrible. And that poor man who jumped—even if he was a Jew—

ROHDE *reacts but says nothing.*

Are you all right? You look sick.

ANNA

Grete, I have a pair of shoes that might fit you—real patent leather, too.

Looking in the closet

Here they are.

She hands them to GRETE.

GRETE

Her face lighting up

Now that's what I call generous!

Starts toward door

If only I had a dress to go with them—

ANNA

Pulling a red dress from the closet

Here's a dress, Grete.

GRETE

Oh, it's gorgeous! I hope it fits.

ANNA

Shepherding her to the door

Why don't you go and try it on.

GRETE

You sound like you want to get rid of me—

Suddenly the sirens wail, announcing another raid.

Another one! What for? The Führer's already dead. Coming to the cellar?

She turns, laughing.

No, of course not.

She leaves. There is a slight pause.

ROHDE

Don't you ever go to the cellar?

ANNA

No—it's like sitting in your own grave, waiting to die, waiting to be covered over.

ROHDE

Going to the bed, starting to pull on his boots

The street will be empty in a few minutes. I can go then.

ANNA

She goes to bed, sits.

Where to?

ROHDE

Somewhere—an empty cellar, the ruins. I'll be all right now.

ANNA

Isn't it safer if you stay here?

ROHDE

Not for you. Grete heard me say I'm leaving tonight. She'll be watching.

ANNA

She has her new dress—that'll keep her busy tonight.

ROHDE

A pause

And tomorrow?

ANNA

Tomorrow?

A pause

Who can think that far ahead?

They look at one another. The first sounds of the bombardment can be heard as the lights dim. In the blackness the noise of the raid can be heard. Then this fades and there is silence.

Curtain

Scene Two

The same, the next morning

Sporadic shell and small-arms fire can be heard. White sheets and towels are displayed as flags at some of the windows visible outside.

ROHDE *is alone, dressed. He stands at the window, looking out at the rubble. Suddenly, the door opens and* KOERNER *enters.*

KOERNER
Frau Walter?
ROHDE
She's not here.
KOERNER
Eying him suspiciously
Where did she go?
ROHDE
No idea.
They stare at one another.
Who are you?
KOERNER
None of your business. Who are you?
ROHDE
None of *your* business.
KOERNER
It is precisely my business—I'm the new block warden.

ROHDE

Oh, so you're Koerner.

KOERNER

How do you know that?

ROHDE

You're a very famous man.

KOERNER

Not sure if ROHDE *is being sarcastic*

You may think you're fooling everybody but you're not. I know you were here last night.

ROHDE

So—?

KOERNER

My orders are to report all unauthorized persons staying in the building—especially soldiers.

Holding his hand out stiffly

Papers please.

ROHDE

Wearily

Tell me something, Koerner. When you said you were the new block warden, how new is new?

KOERNER

Why?

ROHDE

It's a pity the war has to end just as you get a job you like.

KOERNER

You think I like all this extra work?

ROHDE

I think you love it—but it's piling up faster than you can handle. Look out the window, Block Warden. See all those white flags? Towels, bedsheets, anything people can find— that means the Russians are practically around the corner. Are you going to report all of those people, too?

KOERNER

Uncertainly

I—I don't think they belong to my block—

ROHDE

Why don't you get smart and hang out a white flag of your own? You haven't much time, you know.

KOERNER

Never! Doctor Goebbels said any street showing a white flag will be blasted from the map of Berlin. Nobody's getting out so easily.

He moves to the door.

ROHDE

Blocking KOERNER's *exit*

You're so right, Koerner. Nobody's getting out so easily.

KOERNER

Uncertainly

Get—get away from the door—

ROHDE *doesn't move.*

Damn it, this is treason!

ROHDE

Be careful of that word, Koerner. What is treason this morning may not be treason tonight—the traitors arrested yesterday might be national heroes tomorrow.

KOERNER

Nervously

Let me out of here!

ROHDE

As shooting is heard downstairs and KOERNER *turns to the window*

Who's that shooting, Koerner? Germans killing traitors who hung out white flags? Or Russians killing the traitors who didn't? It's a bad day to talk about treason, Block Warden.

KOERNER

Get out of my way!

ROHDE *throws him roughly onto the bed. At this moment* ANNA *enters.* KOERNER, *seeing the open door, makes his break and goes.*

69

ANNA

Erich—what's wrong?

ROHDE

He's going to report me—

ANNA

No he won't. I know the man—he's too corrupt. He'll wait for his bribe.

ROHDE

Sounding hopeful

You think so?

ANNA

Yes. Then he'll report you.

ROHDE

Did he denounce the sergeant on the lamppost?

ANNA

So they say.

ROHDE

And Otto Wilke?

ANNA

No.

A pause; then she turns on a smile with some effort.

Look what I got for us—

She opens the packages she brought back.

We're rich. Bread, butter, and coffee—real coffee. You should have seen what I had to go through to get it. And butter's so scarce they won't even take the coupons any more. I had to give up my last pair of silk stockings for it.

Holds up the bag of coffee

Do you know how long it's been since we've seen *real* coffee?

ROHDE

What did you have to give for that?

ANNA

Aren't you cute! But it just so happens I didn't have to give anything for it—it's a Survivor's Bonus.

ROHDE

A what?

ANNA

Survivor's Bonus—that's what they call it. The party gives out extra rations after the really heavy air raids. You see? We get rewards for being so loyal that we survive the bombs.

ROHDE

That's incredible.

ANNA

But it's true! When ten thousand are killed we get a quarter-pound of sugar—twenty thousand, a quarter-pound of coffee. It's quite a system. You can eat better and keep track of the losses at the same time.

Suddenly

I almost forgot!

She reaches into her purse and pulls out a pack of cigarettes.

Cigarettes!

ROHDE

Hesitating

I'm afraid to ask how many people got killed just so we could smoke—fifty thousand, at least.

ANNA

No, they're black market—I splurged. A pair of earrings.

ROHDE

Anna, you shouldn't have. What if you'd been caught?

ANNA

Lighting his cigarette

Everybody does it—

ROHDE

Coughing

It's going to take time—everything's going to take time. It's like starting life all over again—a cigarette, a bed, a clean shirt, a woman—

Looking at her intently

—especially a woman, it seems—

A pause

Anna—

ANNA

No, please. Don't say anything.

ROHDE

Ignore it, you mean—as if nothing had happened—

ANNA

It's all right, Erich, all right. It wasn't serious—

Smiling

You were very sweet.

ROHDE

Yes, that's right—that's the proper thing to say, isn't it? The generous thing: "There, there—it's all right—you mustn't blame yourself—those things happen sometimes."

ANNA

What are you getting so upset about?

ROHDE

It never happened to me before.

ANNA

Erich, what's the point in discussing it? Whatever happened, happened—or didn't happen—and next time it will be different, that's all.

ROHDE

And suppose it isn't?

ANNA

Shrugging

There's always the priesthood.

ROHDE

It isn't funny, Anna—

ANNA

Why isn't it? If it happened to someone else you'd get a good laugh out of it, all right.

ROHDE

But it didn't happen to someone else!

ANNA

So what? Are you too sacred for jokes? For God's sake,
Erich, what did you expect? After seven years of pain and
fear and loneliness—on a day when you ran for your life,
killed a man, and seriously burned your own flesh—did
you think that life would just begin again exactly where it
had left off?

ROHDE

You're not a man.

ANNA

Christ, I'm sick of male vanity! It's so Goddamned boring!
The phone rings. She puts her hands to her ears.

Oh no! Not another one! Not now!

ROHDE

Anna! What is it?

ANNA

Nearly hysterical

Why can't they leave me alone!

ROHDE

Who, Anna?

ANNA

I tell them there's nothing to be done, but they keep calling
anyway!

ROHDE

He picks up the phone.

Who is this?— What?— Who?

A pause

No—I'm not Otto Wilke— No—he's dead—two years ago
—I'm sorry—I'm sorry—

*He holds the dead phone in his hand for a moment, then
hangs up.*

He sounded so desperate.

73

He sits on the bed.

Anna, who was this Otto Wilke—some sort of a saint?

ANNA

He was a shopkeeper—men's shirts and ties, that sort of thing. He wasn't even opposed to Hitler—not at the beginning. Then he was arrested.

ROHDE

What for? What did he do?

ANNA

Nothing. It was a mistake. He was the wrong Otto Wilke. He was only in jail five days, then they realized their mistake and let him go. He never told me what happened during those five days—not a word. But pretty soon, by ones and twos, men started coming to the apartment, and calling —men like that man on the phone—like you yesterday— men who needed help.

ROHDE

And he helped them.

ANNA

He asked me if I had any objections to what he was doing. I said no, I was glad. I said I'd even help if he wanted. But he wouldn't let me. It was too dangerous, he said.

ROHDE

He was your husband.

ANNA

Yes. Then they came and took him away.

ROHDE

Who betrayed him? Do you know?

ANNA

A pause

I did.

ROHDE

Astounded

What?

ANNA

Yes. I betrayed him.

ROHDE

But—why?

ANNA

He told me to. He insisted—he said it was my only chance. He came home one day and told me there was a traitor in the group—they didn't know who it was, but someone was turning them in. Three of them had already been picked up by the Gestapo. I told him we'd go away but he said it was too late, he was being followed already. He said I'd be arrested, too, if I didn't report him.

She thinks for a moment.

He told me what to say: I had just found out about his activities and it was my duty as a loyal German to report him. He even picked out the dress I should wear. We drank a glass of wine together—sat without saying anything for a while—then he told me to go. When I was out in the street I looked up at our window—that one. I saw his face pressed against the glass—white—his white face smiling— They held me for three hours. When I got back he was gone. I never saw him again. A few weeks later they came and handed me a cigar box with some ashes in it—his ashes, they said—it's hard to recognize ashes. They gave me an extra ration card as a reward for my loyalty—they told me the party was proud of me. They also told me it would be better if I changed my name.

A pause

ROHDE

You still love him, don't you?

ANNA

Flaring up

I hate him! His despicable heroics! "Live," he told me, "live and forget me." "I love you," he said, "and if you love me you'll do what I ask." I loved him enough to do it—but he

75

didn't love me enough to take me with him! "Forget me," he said. But that was the last thing he wanted. He was going to live on in my memory—that's what he wanted! Vanity! Male vanity! So he left me here to receive his ashes in a cigar box and the congratulations of his murderers for a job well done. He left me to answer the phone whenever some poor soul called for help. And he left me with something else, too—something worse—

ROHDE

What else?

ANNA

The uncertainty! Do you think I'll ever be sure—*completely* sure they would have gotten him without my help?

ROHDE

That's why you hit me yesterday—when I said you could save yourself by denouncing me.

ANNA

Twice would be a little ridiculous, don't you think? The coffee should be ready now.

She goes to the stove and pours two cups.

ROHDE

Anna, can you really blame him—for wanting to save you?

ANNA

Blame him? I don't blame him. I blame myself—for going along with it. I was too close to understand.

ROHDE

Understand what?

ANNA

His need for heroics! Men *love* to dream about heroics. On white horses—against impossible odds—to save some helpless woman in distress. It's your eternal, adolescent dream of glory.

ROHDE

And what do women dream about?

ANNA

Reality. Didn't you know that? We only dream about

what's possible. Can you imagine, for instance, that a woman could have conceived of this impossible war—or *any* war? Marching, saluting, killing—what could be more absurd?

ROHDE

Women would have done it all better, I suppose.

ANNA

Why not? We couldn't have done it worse! And don't be condescending—my husband was condescending.

ROHDE

It seems we share a lot of things—

ANNA

All the wrong things.

ROHDE

If I promise not to be condescending—if I promise not to be heroic—would you like me better then?

ANNA

It would help.

A pause

Erich—maybe I could be very grateful that you showed up.

ROHDE

Why?

ANNA

Otto Wilke helped forty-two men escape. If you became the forty-third, I think I could forgive him for what he did to me.

ROHDE

It's nice to know I could be of use to you.

ANNA

You have been already.

ROHDE

Really? How?

ANNA

Laughing

Now Grete knocks before she comes in.

ROHDE

Laughing, too

Is that all?

ANNA

She looks away.

No—

Thinking

This morning, for the first time in two years, I woke up without remembering my nightmares.

ROHDE

He is staring intently at her.

Anna—is it possible that I'm falling in love with you?

ANNA

Love? We barely know each other's name!

ROHDE

So what? Yesterday I didn't even know that you existed. Anna! It's how I feel!

ANNA

But it's nonsense! You've been locked up in a cell too long.

ROHDE

Anna—

ANNA

Gratitude—that's all it is! And desire, of course. If you think it's love now, just wait until your powers return— you'll think it's the romance of the century!

ROHDE

Then you feel nothing at all—

ANNA

I like you. I think you're smart. I think you're brave and strong. I think you're probably good in bed—I'll reserve judgment on that one. But love? No, not yet, Erich.

ROHDE

Not yet? That sounds hopeful.

ANNA

Does it?

ROHDE

As though you thought you could.

As she says nothing

Do you think you ever could, Anna?

ANNA

I don't know. Probably. But that doesn't mean I will.

ROHDE

No, of course not. Loneliness is so much more fun.

ANNA

If I do, Erich—

A pause

—if I do—promise you won't ever leave me.

ROHDE

I won't ever leave you.

ANNA

Promise!

ROHDE

I promise.

He takes her in his arms and kisses her.

ANNA

Still being held, she smiles.

I think you can forget about the priesthood.

Suddenly GRETE *enters without knocking.*

GRETE

Frau Walter—

She stops when she sees ROHDE *and* ANNA, *then remembers to knock. They laugh.*

Don't tell me you're still here.

ROHDE

I was just going.

GRETE

Weren't you supposed to leave last night?

ROHDE

You have a good memory.

ANNA

Where are you going?

ROHDE

I want to have a little talk with Koerner.

He goes.

GRETE

I think it's starting now.

ANNA

What?

GRETE

The baby. Frau Zandler's in labor now.

ANNA

Is she all right?

GRETE

I'm not exactly sure. I've never seen anyone in labor before.

ANNA

I'd better take a look.

GRETE and ANNA leave. The scene remains empty; the sound of shelling and the rattle of a distant machine gun are heard.

Then there is a knock at the door. A moment, then the door opens and SCHMIDT appears. He is now wearing civilian clothes and he carries several packages. He looks around, sees no one, goes to the table and puts down his packages. He checks the closet, stops when he sees the dresses. He fingers them for an instant, then goes to the window and looks out. Next he goes to the bed, tests it with his hand, smiles with satisfaction and stretches out, without removing his shoes, his head propped up on the pillow. Then he notices the radio and turns it on.

RADIO

Warming up

—it is now certain that Doctor Goebbels died with the Führer. There are reports that Martin Bormann is also dead, as well as Gestapo Chief Himmler, but these, as yet, are unconfirmed. Meanwhile, Reichs Marshal Göring—

SCHMIDT *turns off the radio.*

SCHMIDT

Sounds like Wagner's going to get quite a workout.

The door opens. ANNA *is holding it open while speaking to* GRETE *in the hall outside.*

ANNA

Grete, there's no use in calling the midwife now. Stay with her, and let me know if the pains come more regularly.

SCHMIDT

It's comforting to know that some women can behave sensibly in a crisis.

ANNA

Startled

What—what are you doing here?

SCHMIDT

Don't worry—this isn't an official call.

ANNA

What do you want?

SCHMIDT

Why so suspicious? I'm paying a social call—and in the proper manner, too.

Pointing to the packages on the table

Presents. Tell me—has your boy friend left?

ANNA

What boy friend?

SCHMIDT

Your cousin.

ANNA

Nervously

You can see for yourself.

SCHMIDT

Good. Shake hands with your new cousin.

He holds out his hand, but she doesn't respond.

Come, now. You must say I acted decently. After all, he wasn't carrying any papers—I could have had him hanged as a deserter. But what did I do? Nothing. Live and let live is my motto—good luck to him. And, if anyone happened to be grateful—?

ANNA

Gaining confidence

You could have hanged him for all I care. But speaking of deserters—haven't you lost a uniform somewhere?

SCHMIDT

Laughing

Oh, that! Yes, it feels quite strange without it, I must say— as if I were only half dressed.

ANNA

Don't tell me the war's over.

SCHMIDT

Mine is. Aren't you going to open your presents?

He crosses to the table and opens the packages as he speaks.

They weren't easy to come by, let me tell you—not even for me. Scotch whiskey, Swiss cheese, Westphalian ham— look at this—even Beluga caviar!

He reaches into his pocket.

And ration cards—enough for ten to live on—Anna—

ANNA

You remember my name—

SCHMIDT

I know all about you—I've done my homework. But we'll have time for that later on. Right now, let's—

ANNA

Later on?

SCHMIDT

Yes. Didn't I tell you? I live here now—with you.

ANNA

Frightened, but trying not to show it

You must be out of your mind!

SCHMIDT

Yes—from the first moment I saw you.

ANNA

Very touching, but—

SCHMIDT

Taking hold of her

We'll be good for each other, Anna—

ANNA

Let go of me!

SCHMIDT

His manner changing suddenly

Don't play the lady with me. If all the men who'd been in that bed were here now we could hold the Russians off for another year.

ANNA *picks up a bottle from the table and starts to swing at him, but he catches her arm and takes the bottle away.*

Careful—that's real Scotch whiskey.

ANNA

Get out of here!

SCHMIDT

What do you say we open it?

He occupies himself with it.

ANNA

But you can't stay. The Russians will be here soon—

SCHMIDT

I'm sure they will.

ANNA

What will you do then?

SCHMIDT

Greet them with open arms.

ANNA

Laughing

That I'd like to see!

SCHMIDT

Oh, you will. And you'll be rewarded for it, too.

ANNA

For what—hiding a Gestapo officer?

SCHMIDT

No—for hiding an escaped prisoner.

ANNA

Startled

What?

SCHMIDT

Yes, a pathetic victim of a Nazi concentration camp—

A pause as she stares at him anxiously

Me.

ANNA

You?

SCHMIDT

Certainly. Who did you think? Look at these.

He takes some papers from his inside jacket pocket.

An old friend in Registration fixed me up—official, right down to the stamp.

He returns them to his pocket.

ANNA

But how do you know they'll believe you?

SCHMIDT

Papers are everything in this world. Without papers a hero could be taken for a traitor. But with them—

ANNA

A Nazi could be taken for a hero.

SCHMIDT

I wouldn't have put it that way, but that's the general idea. So let the Russians come—I'm safe.

He fills a glass, drinks it, fills it again, and offers it to her.

ANNA

Thinks for a moment, then takes the glass

84

Still, I think you'd be better off somewhere where you aren't known.

SCHMIDT

Where, for instance?

ANNA

In one of the shelters. I understand they're using the subway stations now. There's thousands of people down there —no one will notice you.

SCHMIDT

When the Führer heard the Russians were advancing through the tunnels, he ordered the subways flooded.

ANNA

Shocked

But—all the people—

SCHMIDT *shrugs.*

Oh, no—

SCHMIDT

They say it was the last order he gave. So the subways are out. It was a bad idea, anyway. The Russians will check those places very carefully, but they can't check every single room in the city—can they?

ANNA

Maybe not, but the Russians aren't here yet. And in the meantime, you've picked the wrong building to wait for them in. The super here is the block warden. He'd love to report an escaped prisoner.

SCHMIDT

He'll be glad to have me around—to prove to the Russians he was never a real Nazi.

ANNA

Not this one. He still thinks we'll win the war.

SCHMIDT

One of those. Well, maybe I'd better have a talk with him.

ANNA

Nervously

Yes, but not now. Later.

SCHMIDT

Later? You mean I can stay?

ANNA

Do I have any choice?

SCHMIDT

None whatsoever.

ANNA

In that case—please stay. But I'm going to need a little time. Can you be back in about an hour?

SCHMIDT

Why?

ANNA

I have a few things to arrange.

SCHMIDT

What things?

The door opens and ROHDE *appears.*

Never mind—I see what things.

To ROHDE

Come in, Lieutenant.

Not understanding the situation, ROHDE *hesitates, finally enters, and closes the door.*

Excuse me, I've forgotten your name.

ROHDE

Vollmer. Hans Vollmer.

SCHMIDT

Did you know we're related, Vollmer? That's right, we're cousins now. Once removed. I thought you were leaving last night.

ANNA

He couldn't get away last night.

SCHMIDT

What's the matter? Afraid of the dark?

ANNA

He's leaving now—just stopped by to pick up his things—

ROHDE

Uncertainly

Yes—that's right.

SCHMIDT

I'm afraid the matinee is not as convincing as the evening performance.

ANNA

Going to ROHDE *and pushing him toward the door*

Never mind your things, Hans. I'll keep them for you. Good luck and take care of yourself.

She is pushing him to the door.

ROHDE

Good-bye, Anna.

He opens the door.

SCHMIDT

Producing a gun

Don't go, Lieutenant. Come in and sit down.

To ANNA

Please close the door.

ROHDE *looks at* ANNA, *then follows* SCHMIDT's *directions.*

I'd be very interested in hearing *where* you were going, Lieutenant.

ANNA

What difference does it make?

SCHMIDT

Now that he's seen me here, a great deal of difference, I'm afraid. Where, Vollmer?

ROHDE

Nowhere in particular. I've been cut off from my regiment—and I can't do much fighting with this arm, anyway.

SCHMIDT

Yes, it's a pity about that arm.

ANNA

You'd better stop worrying about his arm and look out for your own neck.

SCHMIDT

That's exactly what I am doing. You were pretty anxious to get rid of him, weren't you?

ANNA

What if I was? I was pretty anxious to get rid of you, too, if you'll remember. Why don't you both clear out? I don't need either of you. You'll make a stunning pair—the Army and the party. You can pass the time telling each other how you both deserted when the going got rough.

SCHMIDT

So he is a deserter.

ROHDE

And what are you—a tourist?

SCHMIDT

What's that supposed to mean?

ROHDE

At least I'm still in uniform. Where'd you get that suit, Group Leader?

SCHMIDT

There are thousands of men's suits in Berlin to which the men are missing, Lieutenant. The suit isn't so important as the papers one carries in the pocket.

Patting his pocket

I have my papers, Vollmer.

ROHDE

They won't do you much good when the Russians come, Group Leader.

SCHMIDT

You still don't understand, do you? The Group Leader's dead. He died two hours ago in an office—very peacefully. Death by pen and ink. You have faith in ultimate justice— you think that because Vollmer's your real name you'll be able to prove it somehow. Forget it. My new name's a hundred times more real than yours because I have the papers to go with it.

ANNA

Don't you think you ought to tell us what your new name is? We can't go on calling you Group Leader—that might embarrass you in front of company.

SCHMIDT

Of course. It's Katz. Joseph Katz.

ROHDE

Shocked

Katz?

SCHMIDT

Smiling

Yes—anything wrong?

ROHDE

You might have given the name a little time to cool off.

SCHMIDT

Why? The real Katz—

Catching himself

—or, rather, the previous Katz—won't object, I promise you. But if he should, there are other names I can use. How do you feel about—Otto Wilke? Do you think that suits me?

ANNA

Stunned

Wilke?

SCHMIDT

Yes, don't you remember him? He was your husband.

No answer from ANNA

An enemy of the party. The denunciation came from someone at this address, didn't it, Frau *Walter?*

ANNA

Yes.

SCHMIDT

You can see I did some checking last night. I wanted to make sure you were loyal to the party.

ANNA

Do you—know what happened to him?

SCHMIDT

The usual—interrogation and heart failure. Tell me, why did you change your name, Frau Wilke?

ROHDE

Why did you change yours, Group Leader?

SCHMIDT

Staring at ROHDE

Yes—and how about you? She's changed her identity. So have I. Have you, Lieutenant?

ROHDE

Hesitating, then smiling

Perhaps.

SCHMIDT

Laughing

Good! It's a marvelous game!

ROHDE

Yes, a marvelous game.

SCHMIDT

Thinking

But I'm afraid your presence here is going to be something of a liability.

ANNA

Yes, that's right. Let him go.

SCHMIDT

It's not that simple. He had his chance to leave last night and he missed it. Now he knows I'm here.

ANNA

Don't be ridiculous! Why should be tell anyone? He'll give you his word—

SCHMIDT

His word? As what? I don't know who he is! If he's a Nazi
he'll turn me in for being out of uniform. If he's an anti-
Nazi he'll turn me in because I *used* to wear the uniform.
Which is to say nothing about a jealous lover thrown out of
bed who'd do it just out of spite.

ANNA

What are you going to do?

SCHMIDT

The Russians are going to be quite impressed with my having killed a German officer singlehanded. So you see, Lieutenant, the only way you can help us is by dying.

ANNA

You wouldn't!

ROHDE

Of course he would. But he won't—not yet.

SCHMIDT

Do you mind telling us why?

ROHDE

Because your premise is wrong. It's true the Russians would
congratulate you for killing a German soldier, but they're
not here yet. And if the Gestapo walks in here first, they
won't even give you a chance to explain—not with those
papers in your pocket.

SCHMIDT

He thinks about it, then lowers the gun and turns to ANNA.

A clever fellow, our cousin.

To ROHDE

You're right, Lieutenant. As long as the Gestapo controls
the street down there you're safe.

ROHDE

So it seems the Gestapo is protecting me after all.

SCHMIDT

Why not? I'm waiting for the Russians to liberate me.

He laughs.

There's no reason why we have to sit around like strangers.
Have a drink, Lieutenant.

*He reaches for the whiskey and fills three glasses. He pushes
one to* ROHDE.

ROHDE

No thanks, Schmidt.

SCHMIDT

The name is Katz.

ROHDE

There doesn't seem much point in my practicing it.

SCHMIDT

For God's sake, Lieutenant, don't be so greedy! You've had
more than most. You've loved and you've killed—there's
really not much more a man can do in this world. So have a
drink, and don't sulk away the rest of your life.

He pushes the glass to ROHDE, *who looks at it a moment,
then drinks it.*

That's right. You, too, Anna—it'll be good for your nerves.

She turns away.

What's wrong? You're worried about him? You'll forget
him soon enough—you'd better. These days, if you can't
forget you've had it. Right, Lieutenant?

ROHDE

No, Schmidt, *not* right.

SCHMIDT

Have it your own way.

A silence; he drinks.

The truth of the matter is I was never a real National
Socialist.

ROHDE

I was wondering when you'd get around to that.

SCHMIDT

Hitler was a fool.

ROHDE

Already?

SCHMIDT

He made some criminal mistakes. We should never have lost this war, but if the Army can hold out for just two more days there won't be a single Nazi left in Germany—we'll all have disappeared underground. We have an obligation to survive—we owe it to Germany.

ANNA

By the window

Look out the window—don't you think you've done enough for Germany?

She looks out.

The Russians must be having difficulties—the white flags are being taken in.

ROHDE

A point for my side.

SCHMIDT

Don't raise your hopes too high, Lieutenant. The Bolsheviks have come all the way from Moscow—this little street isn't going to stop them.

ANNA

It could still take a week.

ROHDE

In that case I think I'll lie down. Waiting to die isn't as exhilarating as it sounds.

He goes to the bed and stretches out, face up, his hands behind his head. A short silence as ANNA *watches him, then turns to* SCHMIDT

ANNA

I think I'll take some of your Scotch whiskey now—

SCHMIDT

Pleased

By all means!

He puts his pistol on the table and fills a glass, handing it to her.

ANNA

Raising her glass to SCHMIDT

Long life.

SCHMIDT

Smiling

Long life.

During this, ROHDE *has slowly reached under the pillow and removed the gun. He now points it at* SCHMIDT.

ROHDE

Schmidt—

SCHMIDT

Turning

I told you not to call me—

He freezes when he sees ROHDE's *gun; then he looks down at his own on the table.*

ROHDE

If you move—if you so much as twitch—I'll blow your head off.

SCHMIDT *stares at* ROHDE's *gun without moving or speaking.*

Anna, take his gun and bring it to me.

He sits up as she follows his orders, never taking his eyes off SCHMIDT *for an instant.* ANNA *brings him the gun.*

All right, Schmidt—

Holding SCHMIDT's *gun in his left hand, he raises his own and aims it at* SCHMIDT.

SCHMIDT

No! What are you doing? Wait—

ROHDE *pulls the trigger and the gun clicks harmlessly.*

It's—*empty?*

ROHDE

I'm afraid so. But, as Anna pointed out, all guns look loaded.

SCHMIDT

I should have killed you. I should have hanged you yesterday when I had the chance!

ROHDE

You'll never have that chance again, I can promise you that.

ANNA

To ROHDE

What are you going to do?

ROHDE

Yes, Schmidt—what *am* I going to do?

SCHMIDT

Nervously

I—I don't know.

ROHDE

Don't you? You were going to shoot me, weren't you?

SCHMIDT *doesn't answer.*

Weren't you?

SCHMIDT

Yes! You see, I admit it. I was trying to save myself—that's
only human, isn't it?

ROHDE

Nothing about you is human.

SCHMIDT

But you've no reason to kill me—it won't help you—I have
the papers—you need me!

ROHDE

Need you, Schmidt? Not if I take your papers—

SCHMIDT

No, you can't. They have *my* picture and *my* fingerprints.
Besides, we're both Germans—we have to stick together
against the foreigners.

ROHDE

Get over by the window.

SCHMIDT

What?

ROHDE

Gesturing with his gun

The window. *Move, Schmidt!*

SCHMIDT

What—what are you going to do?

ROHDE

What do you think?

SCHMIDT

Crossing slowly, playing for time

But—why?

ROHDE

Does it matter? Did you tell Katz why?

SCHMIDT

He was a Jew.

ROHDE

Is that all you knew about him?

SCHMIDT

What else was there?

ROHDE

You've stolen his name—aren't you interested in the man?
He had a face and fingerprints of his own! And a family—
three daughters and a son—

SCHMIDT

Amazed

You *knew* him?

ROHDE

And he knew me.

SCHMIDT

Sinking into a chair

Erich Rohde—

ROHDE

You found me. Aren't you glad? Now get up and move to
that window.

SCHMIDT

Quietly

I don't want to die.

ROHDE

Neither did Katz. He'd be happy to know it's the same room—the same window.

SCHMIDT

No—

ROHDE

Maybe you will make it, Group Leader. Maybe you can fly —the "flower of the nation" can do anything. Can you fly, Schmidt?

SCHMIDT

Terrified

No.

ROHDE

How do you know? Have you ever tried?

SCHMIDT *doesn't answer.*

Have you ever tried?

SCHMIDT

No.

ROHDE

Then try! Get going, Schmidt—out! Show me you have as much courage as a Jew!

SCHMIDT

I've got money—I'll give it to you—

ROHDE

Money?

SCHMIDT

Gold! Not paper—you can have it!

ROHDE

How many wedding rings? How many teeth?

SCHMIDT

To ANNA, *pleading*

Stop him! He's a killer! I was only following orders!

ROHDE

You're talking to the right person now, Schmidt. She be-
lieves survival is the most important thing there is.

SCHMIDT

Yes, that's right! We're all Germans—we'll have to stick
together now—the Jews will make it hard on us—

ROHDE

Jews? What Jews? Are there any left?

SCHMIDT

The Reds—you wait and see! We're all in the same boat, I
tell you!

ANNA

Deliberately, with no emotion

Kill him.

ROHDE

Surprised

What?

ANNA

I said kill him!

A stunned silence

Well? What are you waiting for?

ROHDE

Did you really think I'd do it?

ANNA

What do you mean?

ROHDE

I wasn't going to do it!

ANNA

He has papers—he has the right clothes—he'll get away!

ROHDE

I must find out if that's possible.

ANNA

And if it is? When they take you away, will you ask me to
remember you always?

They regard one another for a moment. Then the door bursts open and GRETE *enters. She is wearing the red dress.*

GRETE

Have you seen them?

ANNA

Who?

GRETE

The Russians! They're outside!

Before anyone can stop him, SCHMIDT, *who has had his back to the window during the above, now turns and shouts outside.*

SCHMIDT

Help! Tovarisch! Tovarisch! Up here! Help!

ROHDE *grabs him, pulls him back into the room, away from the window, and aims his gun at him.*

ROHDE

You bastard! They're too late to save you!

SCHMIDT

No, *you're* too late! They're here! We've got to stick together now or we're all done for!

GRETE *has gone to the window.*

ROHDE

To GRETE

Did they hear him?

GRETE

They must have—they're coming in.

Turning back

What's been going on in here?

SCHMIDT

We'll be all right if you'll just listen to me. I know these people—I know how their minds work. You've got to trust me! I'll tell them you were hiding me, protecting me from the Nazis. It'll work, I tell you—I promise it will work!

ROHDE

Finally

All right, Schmidt, we'll trust you—

ANNA

Are you crazy?

ROHDE

—on one condition. Burn those phony papers.

SCHMIDT

Burn—? But we need them! We'll have to show them something. You don't know them—they're intimidated by papers. But we'll have to get rid of the guns—both of them.

ROHDE

Looking around

Where?

SCHMIDT

He has taken over.

The water tank over the toilet. Give them to me!

ROHDE

She'll do it. You stay here with me.

ANNA *takes the guns and goes into the bathroom.*

SCHMIDT

Remember—leave them to me. But above all, let's trust one another. We're Germans and they're the enemy. Don't forget that.

ANNA *returns.*

GRETE

Smoothing down her dress

At least they can't find fault with the color—

The door flies open and two Russians—a SOLDIER *and a* SERGEANT—*enter, each holding a short, lightweight machine pistol ready to fire. They look not unlike the two German noncoms seen in Scene One—the* SOLDIER *large, forbidding, slow of mind; the* SERGEANT *smaller, shrewd, and humorless.*

SERGEANT

Nobody move! Stand where you are, hands in the air!

There is total silence as each side surveys the other.

Watch them, Stepan Ivanitch. I look next door.

He goes. The silence continues. The SOLDIER *has now confined his gaze to* ROHDE.

SOLDIER

Soldier. Kill Russians?

ROHDE

No.

ANNA

He's not a soldier—he's only—

SCHMIDT

Quiet!

SOLDIER

To SCHMIDT

You Nazi?

SCHMIDT

No. Tovarisch.

SOLDIER

Tovarisch?

SCHMIDT

Yes.

SOLDIER

Looking around

Everyone tovarisch?

SCHMIDT

Yes—tovarisch.

To the OTHERS

Everybody say it—

OTHERS

Tovarisch.

GRETE

What the hell does it mean?

SCHMIDT

Friend.

GRETE

Quickly

Tovarisch, tovarisch!

SOLDIER

If everyone tovarisch, who kill Russians?

He grins.

You have wristwatch?

SCHMIDT

Yes—wristwatch—here—

He quickly unstraps his watch and hands it to him.

SOLDIER

Holding the gun under his arm, he pulls back his sleeve revealing four or five watches already there. He straps on the new one, then turns to ROHDE.

Wristwatch?

ROHDE

Showing his bare wrist

No. Sorry—

SOLDIER

To GRETE

Wristwatch?

GRETE

No. Does that mean I'll be raped?

SOLDIER

Uncomprehending

What?

GRETE

Raped. You know, *raped?*

The SOLDIER *merely shrugs.*

He doesn't know anything.

The SERGEANT *returns.*

SERGEANT

Shouting from window—it came from here?

SCHMIDT

Yes, Sergeant.

SERGEANT

Why?

SCHMIDT

He looks at ROHDE *and* ANNA; *suddenly he points at* ROHDE.

He's a Nazi! He was trying to kill me!

ANNA

Horrified

What?

SCHMIDT

It's true! He would have killed me if you hadn't come!

ANNA

Trust each other! Stick together! Liar! *Liar!*

SERGEANT

Be quiet.

ANNA

I won't! He's a liar!

SERGEANT

Be quiet!

To SCHMIDT

Why he want to kill you?

SCHMIDT

I escaped from a concentration camp yesterday. He's a Nazi.

SERGEANT

To ROHDE

True?

ANNA

No!

SERGEANT

I ask him!

To ROHDE

You are Nazi?

ROHDE

No.

SCHMIDT

What do you expect him to say?

ROHDE

I escaped from prison yesterday.

SERGEANT

Both escape?

SCHMIDT

Don't listen to him!

ANNA

Indicating SCHMIDT

It's him—he's the Nazi!

SERGEANT

Cocking his gun

Be quiet!

He looks at the four Germans for a moment, then speaks to GRETE.

Which one is telling truth?

GRETE

Looking at ROHDE, *then at* SCHMIDT; *the situation is obviously too much for her.*

I don't know.

SERGEANT

Examines both ROHDE *and* SCHMIDT. *Finally he turns to the* SOLDIER.

Shoot them both.

He turns and starts out.

SCHMIDT

No! Wait! Look—I have papers!

He holds out his papers to the SERGEANT. *The* SERGEANT *takes the papers and begins reading them.*

ANNA

They're false! His name's Schmidt! He's with the Gestapo—

SERGEANT

Without looking up

Be quiet!

Now he turns to ROHDE.

Papers?

SCHMIDT

He doesn't have any!

SERGEANT

No papers? Then where is number?

ROHDE

What?

SERGEANT

Number on arm. Show me.

ROHDE

I—I can't. I burned it off—

SERGEANT

To SCHMIDT

You—show number.

SCHMIDT

Hesitating; then

Yes, of course.

He unbuttons his sleeve and reveals a tattoo.

Here it is.

SERGEANT

Good.

ANNA

No! He must have done it to himself—don't you understand? To himself!

SERGEANT

To the SOLDIER, *indicating* ROHDE

Shoot that one.

ANNA

No! You can't! He's innocent!

SERGEANT

He is Nazi.

ANNA

No! He's not a Nazi!

SERGEANT

Then is being shot by mistake.

As the SOLDIER *raises his machine gun, a uniformed Russian* CAPTAIN *enters.*

CAPTAIN

Stop. Lower your gun.

Everyone turns to look at him. The CAPTAIN *is young— thirty-two—slim and fair. He is well-educated, speaking fluent German. He walks to the* SERGEANT, *who, like the* SOLDIER, *stands at rigid attention.*

I have listened to your interrogation, Sergeant—it is unsatisfactory. We are *fighting* fascists, not imitating them. I am Captain Korovkin. If you are innocent you have nothing to be afraid of.

To GRETE

You—come here.

GRETE

I know—you want to rape me. I expected it—

CAPTAIN

Do you live here?

GRETE

Next door—with Frau Zandler.

CAPTAIN

Then go back there, please.

GRETE

The radio *said* you people couldn't be trusted!

And she leaves, closing the door behind her.

CAPTAIN

You and you—step forward.

ROHDE *and* SCHMIDT *approach.*

You will both have a chance to speak.

To ROHDE

You first.

ROHDE

My name is Erich Rohde. I have spent the last seven years in a Nazi concentration camp.

CAPTAIN

Why?

ROHDE

Political reasons.

CAPTAIN

Communist?

ROHDE

No.

CAPTAIN

Go on, please.

ROHDE

Yesterday morning we were ordered shot. I escaped.

CAPTAIN

Pointing to SCHMIDT

Who is he?

ROHDE

Gestapo Group Leader Schmidt. Yesterday he killed a Jew named Joseph Katz.

CAPTAIN

Thank you.

To SCHMIDT

Now you.

SCHMIDT

My name is Joseph Katz. I have spent the last seven years in a Nazi concentration camp.

CAPTAIN

Why?

SCHMIDT

I am Jewish. Yesterday morning we were ordered shot. I
escaped.

CAPTAIN

Pointing to ROHDE

Who is he?

SCHMIDT

Gestapo Group Leader Schmidt. Yesterday he killed a man
named Erich Rohde.

CAPTAIN

Thank you.

He thinks for a moment.

Is there any reason why I should believe you instead of
him?

SCHMIDT

Yes, Captain. I have papers.

He hands his papers to the CAPTAIN.

CAPTAIN

Examining them

Joseph Katz.

He hands them back.

They are in order.

He turns to ROHDE.

Have you anything to say before we shoot you?

ROHDE

A pause; calmly

Captain, who would have the papers? The man in prison?
Or the one who put him there?

SCHMIDT

Realizing the effect of ROHDE'S *words*

What's he talking about?

Looking around

He's so desperate he'll say anything!

He laughs, but not too convincingly.

It's laughable!

The CAPTAIN *walks to the door, opens it wide, and returns to a chair in the center of the room, where he sits.* SCHMIDT *has not taken his eyes from the* CAPTAIN.

Why—did you do that?

The CAPTAIN, *the* SERGEANT, *and the* SOLDIER *stare at* SCHMIDT. *A long silence as they seem to be waiting for something.* SCHMIDT *avoids the three pairs of eyes staring at him; he begins speaking, slowly, waiting after each phrase for some reaction before continuing.*

I'm innocent—
I haven't done anything—
I was a prisoner—
My name is Joseph Katz—
I have papers—
I'm Jewish—
I'm a dirty Jewish swine—
I'm innocent—

Everyone is staring at him. Suddenly he breaks for the open door and runs out. Without a word from anyone, the SOLDIER *fires his machine pistol through the open doorway. A silence follows.*

CAPTAIN

To ROHDE

You can relax now—you won't be shot.

A pause; suddenly ANNA *runs to* ROHDE. *They hold each other in their arms.*

ANNA

Erich—Erich—

ROHDE

Quietly

It's all right now. Everything's all right.

ANNA

I almost lost you.

ROHDE

Don't cry, Anna—laugh! It's over—for us the war's finally over!

ANNA

I can't believe it!

They cling to each other as the CAPTAIN *waits patiently.*

CAPTAIN

Finally, to ROHDE

Excuse me—but why did they put you in prison?

ROHDE

Something I wrote—a letter to a newspaper.

CAPTAIN

And what did your letter say?

ROHDE

It asked if the stories I'd heard were true—that people were being exterminated.

CAPTAIN

And if you'd learned they were true—before you were arrested—what would you have done?

ROHDE

Demanded an explanation, of course!

CAPTAIN

Yes, of course. Not action—merely an explanation. The favorite solution of all reactionaries.

ROHDE

Reactionary? They put me in prison for being a liberal!

CAPTAIN

Smiling

What is wet for the cat is dry for the fish.

Studying him

What is your profession?

ROHDE

I was a writer.

CAPTAIN

Good, very good. It is a fortunate meeting.

ROHDE

Why's that?

CAPTAIN

We have been ordered to look for such people—writers, teachers, intellectuals. Tell me, what is your concept of a new Germany?

ROHDE

What new Germany?

CAPTAIN

A people's Germany—a workers' Germany.

ROHDE

A Communist Germany.

CAPTAIN

Yes. What is your opinion, please?

ROHDE

A pause

Does my opinion matter?

CAPTAIN

Yes, very much. You are intelligent, courageous, articulate. We are offering opportunities to men like you.

ROHDE

Doing what?

CAPTAIN

Helping us to rebuild, to educate. The young need training —the old need retraining.

ROHDE

Indoctrination, you mean?

CAPTAIN

If you like.

ROHDE

Yes, well, if it's all the same to you, I'd rather do something else.

CAPTAIN

You will explain, please.

111

ROHDE

I don't believe in your system.

CAPTAIN

Why not?

ROHDE

I'm against dictatorship.

CAPTAIN

A pause

And just what is it that you do believe in?

ROHDE

What every prisoner comes to believe in—freedom.

CAPTAIN

Freedom. That's not a word that belongs to any of us, not yet. It's a word for the future. Someday, freedom—but for now, hard work, sacrifice, dedication.

ANNA

But you're young—is that all you want from life? Don't you want to be happy?

CAPTAIN

I am unimportant. Only the future of world socialism is important.

ANNA

You can't believe that.

CAPTAIN

Please! You can accuse me of anything you like, but I am not a fool! I am not a—a parrot, repeating slogans—I *believe!* I believe that what we are doing is right—not comfortable, not profitable, not amusing—but *right!* I believe it will benefit not only Russia but the entire world, *including* Germany!

ROHDE

The only thing that will benefit Germany is freedom.

CAPTAIN

The last time Germany had freedom you elected Adolf Hitler.

ROHDE

A pause

Don't you think we've paid for that mistake?

CAPTAIN

Angry

You paid? Have you seen *our* country? Our cities destroyed, our farms burned, our families slaughtered—*we* paid for your mistake, too!

ANNA

But he didn't support them—he was against them!

CAPTAIN

I recognize that. That's why I offer him preferential treatment.

ROHDE

I don't want it! Treat me like the others!

CAPTAIN

Like your friend lying in the hall?

ROHDE

A beat

I'm sorry—I have to refuse.

CAPTAIN

You cannot refuse.

ROHDE

I have no choice?

CAPTAIN

None.

ROHDE

Don't I have any rights?

CAPTAIN

We give you the right to help rebuild your country!

ROHDE

In your image.

CAPTAIN

Of course! We won the war, why shouldn't we? Our image is right. We believe in it.

ROHDE

And I don't—it's as simple as that!

CAPTAIN

You will have to go with the tide!

ROHDE

No! That's what I did the last time! I went with the tide until it was too late! I'll never do it again!

ANNA

Nervously

Erich—

ROHDE

No! I will not help them! I won't even sit back and watch them—not again!

ANNA

Erich—maybe it's different this time.

ROHDE

It's *not* different! They don't permit opposition, and that makes them just as bad as the Nazis!

CAPTAIN

A pause; his manner changes.

Very well. In that case you will come with me, please.

ANNA

Surprised

What do you mean?

CAPTAIN

Since he will not co-operate, he must receive guidance.

ANNA

I—I don't understand. You want him to go somewhere?

CAPTAIN

We have places for education.

ROHDE

So did the Nazis—I just escaped from one!

CAPTAIN

You escaped from a concentration camp. You are going to an information center.

ANNA

For how long?

CAPTAIN

That will depend on him. Until he learns.

To ROHDE

Get your belongings, please.

ROHDE *doesn't move at first. Then the* SERGEANT *steps forward and cocks his gun.*

ROHDE

Yes—my belongings—

He goes to the cupboard and retrieves his prison clothes.

CAPTAIN

Hurry, please!

ANNA

No, wait! Erich—you can't go. You promised you'd stay!

ROHDE

Yes, I know, but I was mistaken.

ANNA

Have you gone insane? Say something! You can still do what he wants—it's not too late!

ROHDE

Don't you understand, Anna? I can't do it again!

ANNA

Why not? Is it so difficult to say "I believe"? Say it, Erich— that's all you have to do!

ROHDE

But I *don't* believe.

ANNA

Then don't—but *say* it! Stop trying to be a martyr! No one remembers martyrs any more—there are too many of them. There are only those who survive and those who don't. He's stronger than you are now. Don't force him to prove it— because in the meantime you have a life, Erich, your only life—*our* only life! What good will you be to anyone back in prison?

ROHDE

What good will I be if I compromise my principles?

ANNA

Keep your principles—but don't die for them! Live for them! Your chance will come someday, but not if you throw your life away. Use your head, Erich. What good are heroics if they can't accomplish anything? It's pointless, Erich, because in the end you will still have to say "I believe." So say it now, for God's sake! And you can say it, Erich—you can say "I believe" just as easily as you can say "I promise I'll never leave you"!

ROHDE

I *can't*, Anna! It's the one thing I learned in these seven years. I can't. I'm sorry.

ANNA

Sorry? It's not enough! *I was better off before!*

She bursts into tears, sobbing convulsively. He holds her, trying to comfort her.

ROHDE

Anna, I'll come back—I'll come back—

When she has been calmed, he releases her. Then he turns, looks at the Russians, nods, and they go.

ANNA's back has been to the door. When she hears it close, she wheels to look at it. Then she lights a cigarette, goes to the window and looks down at the street.

Finally, she turns back to the room, stares at it, then pulls the curtain, darkening the room; next she goes to the bed, lies down, and smokes her cigarette.

Final Curtain

C33772

Stone, Peter, 1930–
    Full circle; a play by Erich Maria Remarque, as adapted
by Peter Stone. New York, Harcourt Brace Jovanovich
[1974]

    viii, 116 p. 22 cm.

    Adapted from E. M. Remarque's Die lezte Station.

    I. Remarque, Erich Maria, 1898–1970. Die lezte Station.
II. Title.

    PS3569.T6416F8   812'.5'4   74–1190
    ISBN 0-15-134100-1 ; 0-15-634020-8 (pbk.)   i 6/09   MARC

o 7/87

IL